The Essential
Keto Diet Cookbook

1200 Low-Carb, High-Fat Recipes Perfect for Busy People on the Keto Diet (BONUS: Stress-free 21-Day Keto Diet Planner)

Daniel D. Becraft

CONTENTS

Chapter 3 Vegan, Vegetable & Meatless Recipes 23

Chapter 4 Poultry Recipes 36

Chapter 7 Soups, Stew & Salads Recipes 76

Chapter 8 Desserts And Drinks Recipes 89

INTRODUCTION

Hello, my name is Daniel D. Becraft, I'm a food blogger, recipe developer and social media influencer. I'm so glad you're willing to learn about and learn from this keto diet cookbook. Whether you just bought the Keto Diet Cookbook or have been using it for years, this beautiful and unique food book will always give you some food inspiration. When some people read this book for the first time, they think it is the kind of recipe book that looks easy but is extremely difficult to make. After all, it contains 1,200 keto recipes. It is easy to give people an illusion: there must be various expensive appliances or extremely complicated steps involved. But when you actually read it, you realize that this is a very practical and creative cooking primer. The content of the book is extremely detailed and clear. It includes a variety of appetizers, snacks, and side dish recipes, vegan, vegetable & meatless recipes and more that can be easily prepared at home. For those who have no cooking experience at all, this book will be an incomparable introductory guide. And for those who want to further improve their cooking skills, this book will also help you broaden your cooking horizons and provide you with unlimited cooking.

This keto diet cookbook has been carefully written to meet the needs of everyone who enjoys cooking and living a healthy life. It was created to serve as a one-stop shop for home cooks to effortlessly prepare delicious keto diet recipes. This cookbook first briefly introduces the main content and benefits of the keto diet, which can quickly help inexperienced people easily master the ketogenic diet. In this book, we'll explore a variety of simple and delicious keto diet recipes. Once you try these delicious treats from the keto diet recipes, you won't regret your purchase. Hope you enjoy cooking with it! all the best!

Chapter 1 Basic Information of Keto Diet

What Exactly Is The Keto Diet?

A keto diet generally refers to a diet that is very low in carbs, moderate in protein, and high in fat. It is effective in weight loss and certain health diseases like diabetes, cancer. It involves drastically reducing your carbohydrate intake and replacing them with fat. The keto diet is not just for weight loss, it is a healthy lifestyle. The advantage of this diet is that it prompts the body to convert from sugar metabolism to fat metabolism, so as to more effectively consume the body's own stored calories.

Why Are More And More People Following The Keto Diet?

The popularity of the keto diet is mainly due to its "low sugar, low carbohydrate and high protein" concept, which is in line with the popular healthy diet trend, creating a natural and healthy image. It's often considered a more sustainable weight loss plan because fat and protein are known to increase satiety, keeping you full and satisfied for longer periods of time.

What To Eat On A Keto Diet?

The keto diet is actually very simple. The main principle is to eat less food rich in sugar and carbohydrates, increase protein appropriately, and take in a high proportion of good fats.

Eat at most meals

• High-quality fats: Olive oil, coconut oil, tallow, avocado oil

• Poultry and their offal: Chicken, duck, goose, beef, sheep

• Eggs: Chicken, duck, goose, quail

• Vegetables that don't contain a lot of starch: Celery, cucumbers, mushrooms, etc.

• Fruit: Avocado

• Drinks: Water, black coffee, green tea, apple cider vinegar, lemonade

Foods to avoid

• All sugary foods and drinks

• All grains

• Vegetables high in starch

• Various wines and alcoholic beverages

• Soy products and sauces

The Health Benefits of the Keto Diet

1. A low-carb, high-fat ketogenic diet is good for weight loss.

2. It is particularly effective in treating and defending against chronic diseases.

3. Helps reduce blood sugar levels.

4. Beneficial in improving insulin resistance.

5. Effectively control epilepsy symptoms.

6. Helps increase HDL content and reduce the risk of heart disease.

Measurement Conversions

BASIC KITCHEN CONVERSIONS & EQUIVALENTS

DRY MEASUREMENTS CONVERSION CHART

3 TEASPOONS = 1 TABLESPOON = 1/16 CUP

6 TEASPOONS = 2 TABLESPOONS = 1/8 CUP

12 TEASPOONS = 4 TABLESPOONS = 1/4 CUP

24 TEASPOONS = 8 TABLESPOONS = 1/2 CUP

36 TEASPOONS = 12 TABLESPOONS = 3/4 CUP

48 TEASPOONS = 16 TABLESPOONS = 1 CUP

METRIC TO US COOKING CONVERSIONS

OVEN TEMPERATURES

120 °C = 250 °F

160 °C = 320 °F

180° C = 350 °F

205 °C = 400 °F

220 °C = 425 °F

LIQUID MEASUREMENTS CONVERSION CHART

8 FLUID OUNCES = 1 CUP = 1/2 PINT = 1/4 QUART

16 FLUID OUNCES = 2 CUPS = 1 PINT = 1/2 QUART

32 FLUID OUNCES = 4 CUPS = 2 PINTS = 1 QUART
 = 1/4 GALLON

128 FLUID OUNCES = 16 CUPS = 8 PINTS = 4 QUARTS = 1 GALLON

BAKING IN GRAMS

1 CUP FLOUR = 140 GRAMS

1 CUP SUGAR = 150 GRAMS

1 CUP POWDERED SUGAR = 160 GRAMS

1 CUP HEAVY CREAM = 235 GRAMS

VOLUME

1 MILLILITER = 1/5 TEASPOON

5 ML = 1 TEASPOON

15 ML = 1 TABLESPOON

240 ML = 1 CUP OR 8 FLUID OUNCES

1 LITER = 34 FL. OUNCES

WEIGHT

1 GRAM = .035 OUNCES

100 GRAMS = 3.5 OUNCES

500 GRAMS = 1.1 POUNDS

1 KILOGRAM = 35 OUNCES

US TO METRIC COOKING CONVERSIONS

1/5 TSP = 1 ML

1 TSP = 5 ML

1 TBSP = 15 ML

1 FL OUNCE = 30 ML

1 CUP = 237 ML

1 PINT (2 CUPS) = 473 ML

1 QUART (4 CUPS) = .95 LITER

1 GALLON (16 CUPS) = 3.8 LITERS

1 OZ = 28 GRAMS

1 POUND = 454 GRAMS

BUTTER

1 CUP BUTTER = 2 STICKS = 8 OUNCES = 230 GRAMS = 8 TABLESPOONS

WHAT DOES 1 CUP EQUAL

1 CUP = 8 FLUID OUNCES

1 CUP = 16 TABLESPOONS

1 CUP = 48 TEASPOONS

1 CUP = 1/2 PINT

1 CUP = 1/4 QUART

1 CUP = 1/16 GALLON

1 CUP = 240 ML

BAKING PAN CONVERSIONS

1 CUP ALL-PURPOSE FLOUR = 4.5 OZ

1 CUP ROLLED OATS = 3 OZ 1 LARGE EGG = 1.7 OZ

1 CUP BUTTER = 8 OZ 1 CUP MILK = 8 OZ

1 CUP HEAVY CREAM = 8.4 OZ

1 CUP GRANULATED SUGAR = 7.1 OZ

1 CUP PACKED BROWN SUGAR = 7.75 OZ

1 CUP VEGETABLE OIL = 7.7 OZ

1 CUP UNSIFTED POWDERED SUGAR = 4.4 OZ

BAKING PAN CONVERSIONS

9-INCH ROUND CAKE PAN = 12 CUPS

10-INCH TUBE PAN =16 CUPS

11-INCH BUNDT PAN = 12 CUPS

9-INCH SPRINGFORM PAN = 10 CUPS

9 X 5 INCH LOAF PAN = 8 CUPS

9-INCH SQUARE PAN = 8 CUPS

Chapter 2 Appetizers, Snacks & Side Dishes Recipes

Parmesan Crackers With Guacamole

Servings: 4 | Cooking Time: 10 Minutes

Ingredients:

- 1 cup finely grated Parmesan cheese
- ¼ tsp sweet paprika
- ¼ tsp garlic powder
- 2 soft avocados, pitted and scooped
- 1 tomato, chopped
- Salt to taste

Directions:

1. To make the chips, preheat oven to 350ºF and line a baking sheet with parchment paper.
2. Mix parmesan cheese, paprika, and garlic powder. Spoon 8 teaspoons on the baking sheet creating spaces between each mound. Flatten mounds. Bake for 5 minutes, cool, and remove to a plate.
3. To make the guacamole, mash avocado, with a fork in a bowl, add in tomato and continue to mash until mostly smooth. Season with salt. Serve crackers with guacamole.

Nutrition Info:

- Per Servings 2g Carbs, 10g Protein, 20g Fat, 229 Calories

Buttered Broccoli

Servings: 6 | Cooking Time: 10 Minutes

Ingredients:

- 1 broccoli head, florets only
- Salt and black pepper to taste
- ¼ cup butter

Directions:

1. Place the broccoli in a pot filled with salted water and bring to a boil. Cook for about 3 minutes.
2. Melt the butter in a microwave. Drain the broccoli and transfer to a plate. Drizzle the butter over and season with some salt and pepper.

Nutrition Info:

- Per Servings 5.5g Carbs, 3.9g Protein, 7.8g Fat, 114 Calories

Bacon-wrapped Jalapeño Peppers

Servings: 6 | Cooking Time: 30 Minutes

Ingredients:

- 12 jalapeños
- ¼ cup shredded colby cheese
- 6 oz cream cheese, softened
- 6 slices bacon, halved

Directions:

1. Cut the jalapeno peppers in half, and then remove the membrane and seeds. Combine cheeses and stuff into the pepper halves. Wrap each pepper with a bacon strip and secure with toothpicks.
2. Place the filled peppers on a baking sheet lined with a piece of foil. Bake at 350ºF for 25 minutes until bacon has browned, and crispy and cheese is golden brown on the top. Remove to a paper towel lined plate to absorb grease, arrange on a serving plate, and serve warm.

Nutrition Info:

- Per Servings 0g Carbs, 14g Protein, 17g Fat, 206 Calories

Herb Cheese Sticks

Servings: 4 | Cooking Time: 15 Minutes

Ingredients:

- 1 cup pork rinds, crushed
- 1 tbsp Italian herb mix
- 1 egg
- 1 lb swiss cheese, cut into sticks
- Cooking spray

Directions:

1. Preheat oven to 350ºF and line a baking sheet with parchment paper. Combine pork rinds and herb mix in a bowl to be evenly mixed and beat the egg in another bowl. Coat the cheese sticks in egg and then generously dredge in pork rind mixture. Arrange on baking sheet. Bake for 4 to 5 minutes, take out after, let cool for 2 minutes, and serve with marinara sauce.

Nutrition Info:

- Per Servings 0g Carbs, 8g Protein, 17.3g Fat, 188 Calories

Coconut And Chocolate Bars

Servings: 6 | Cooking Time: 30 Minutes

Ingredients:

- 1 tbsp Stevia
- ¾ cup shredded coconut, unsweetened
- ½ cup ground nuts (almonds, pecans, or walnuts)
- ¼ cup unsweetened cocoa powder
- 4 tbsp coconut oil
- Done

Directions:

1. In a medium bowl, mix shredded coconut, nuts, and cocoa powder.
2. Add Stevia and coconut oil.
3. Mix batter thoroughly.
4. In a 9x9 square inch pan or dish, press the batter and for a 30-minutes place in the freezer.
5. Serve and enjoy.

Nutrition Info:

- Per Servings 2.3g Carbs, 1.6g Protein, 17.8g Fat, 200 Calories

Italian-style Chicken Wraps

Servings: 8 | Cooking Time: 20 Minutes

Ingredients:

- ¼ tsp garlic powder
- 8 ounces provolone cheese
- 8 raw chicken tenders
- Salt and black pepper to taste
- 8 prosciutto slices

Directions:

1. Pound the chicken until half an inch thick. Season with salt, black pepper, and garlic powder. Cut the provolone cheese into 8 strips. Place a slice of prosciutto on a flat surface. Place one chicken tender on top. Top with a provolone strip.
2. Roll the chicken and secure with previously soaked skewers. Grill the wraps for 3 minutes per side.

Nutrition Info:

- Per Servings 0.7g Carbs, 17g Protein, 10g Fat, 174 Calories

Keto "cornbread"

Servings: 8 | Cooking Time: 30 Minutes

Ingredients:

- 1 ¼ cups coconut milk
- 4 eggs, beaten
- 4 tbsp baking powder
- ½ cup almond meal
- 3 tablespoons olive oil

Directions:

1. Prepare 8 x 8-inch baking dish or a black iron skillet then add shortening.
2. Put the baking dish or skillet inside the oven on 425oF and leave there for 10 minutes.
3. In a bowl, add coconut milk and eggs then mix well. Stir in the rest of the ingredients.
4. Once all ingredients are mixed, pour the mixture into the heated skillet.
5. Then cook for 15 to 20 minutes in the oven until golden brown.

Nutrition Info:

- Per Servings 2.6g Carbs, 5.4g Protein, 18.9g Fat, 196 Calories

Jalapeno Popper Spread

Servings: 8 | Cooking Time: 3 Mins

Ingredients:

- 2 packages cream cheese, softened; low-carb
- 1 cup. mayonnaise
- 1 can chopped green chilies, drained
- 2 ounces canned diced jalapeno peppers, drained
- 1 cup. grated Parmesan cheese

Directions:

1. Combine cream cheese and mayonnaise in a bowl until incorporated. Add in jalapeno peppers and green chilies. In a microwave safe bowl, spread jalapeno peppers mixture and sprinkle with Parmesan cheese.
2. Microwave jalapeno peppers mixture on High about 3 minutes or until warm.

Nutrition Info:

- Per Servings 1g Carbs, 2.1g Protein, 11.1g Fat, 110 Calories

Pesto Stuffed Mushrooms

Servings: 6 | Cooking Time: 25 Minutes

Ingredients:

- 6 large cremini mushrooms
- 6 bacon slices
- 2 tablespoons basil pesto
- 5 tablespoons low-fat cream cheese softened

Directions:

1. Line a cookie sheet with foil and preheat oven to 375oF.
2. In a small bowl mix well, pesto and cream cheese.
3. Remove stems of mushrooms and discard. Evenly fill mushroom caps with pesto-cream cheese filling.
4. Get one stuffed mushroom and a slice of bacon. Wrap the bacon all over the mushrooms. Repeat process on remaining mushrooms and bacon.
5. Place bacon-wrapped mushrooms on prepared pan and bake for 25 minutes or until bacon is crispy.
6. Let it cool, evenly divide into suggested servings, and enjoy.

Nutrition Info:

- Per Servings 2.0g Carbs, 5.0g Protein, 12.2g Fat, 137.8 Calories

Reese Cups

Servings: 12 | Cooking Time: 1 Minute

Ingredients:

- ¼ cup unsweetened shredded coconut
- 1 cup almond butter
- ½ cup dark chocolate chips
- 1 tablespoon Stevia
- 1 tablespoon coconut oil

Directions:

1. Line 12 muffin tins with 12 muffin liners.
2. Place the almond butter, honey, and oil in a glass bowl and microwave for 30 seconds or until melted. Divide the mixture into 12 muffin tins. Let it cool for 30 minutes in the fridge.
3. Add the shredded coconuts and mix until evenly distributed.
4. Pour the remaining melted chocolate on top of the coconuts. Freeze for an hour.
5. Carefully remove the chocolates from the muffin tins to create perfect Reese cups.
6. Serve and enjoy.

Nutrition Info:

- Per Servings 10.7g Carbs, 5.0g Protein, 17.1g Fat, 214 Calories

Garlic Flavored Kale Taters

Servings: 4 | Cooking Time: 20 Minutes

Ingredients:

- 4 cups kale, rinsed and chopped
- 2 cups cauliflower florets, finely chopped
- 2 tbsp almond milk
- 1 clove of garlic, minced
- 3 tablespoons oil
- 1/8 teaspoon black pepper
- cooking spray

Directions:

1. Heat oil in a large skillet and sauté the garlic for 2 minutes. Add the kale until it wilts. Transfer to a large bowl.
2. Add the almond milk. Season with pepper to taste.
3. Evenly divide into 4 and form patties.
4. Lightly grease a baking pan with cooking spray. Place patties on pan. Place pan on the top rack of the oven and broil on low for 6 minutes. Turnover patties and cook for another 4 minutes.
5. Serve and enjoy.

Nutrition Info:

- Per Servings 5g Carbs, 2g Protein, 11g Fat, 117 Calories

Cardamom And Cinnamon Fat Bombs

Servings: 10 | Cooking Time: 3 Minutes

Ingredients:

- ¼ tsp ground cardamom (green)
- ¼ tsp ground cinnamon
- ½ cup unsweetened shredded coconut
- ½ tsp vanilla extract
- 3-oz unsalted butter, room temperature

Directions:

1. Place a nonstick pan on medium fire and toast coconut until lightly browned.
2. In a bowl, mix all ingredients.
3. Evenly roll into 10 equal balls.
4. Let it cool in the fridge.
5. Serve and enjoy.

Nutrition Info:

- Per Servings 0.4g Carbs, 0.4g Protein, 10.0g Fat, 90 Calories

Curry ' N Poppy Devilled Eggs

Servings: 6 | Cooking Time: 8 Minutes

Ingredients:

- ½ cup mayonnaise
- ½ tbsp poppy seeds
- 1 tbsp red curry paste
- 6 eggs
- ¼ tsp salt

Directions:

1. Place eggs in a small pot and add enough water to cover it. Bring to a boil without a cover, lower fire to a simmer and simmer for 8 minutes.
2. Immediately dunk in ice-cold water once done the cooking. Peel eggshells and slice eggs in half lengthwise.
3. Remove yolks and place them in a medium bowl. Add the rest of the ingredients in the bowl except for the egg whites. Mix well.
4. Evenly return the yolk mixture into the middle of the egg whites.
5. Serve and enjoy.

Nutrition Info:

- Per Servings 1.0g Carbs, 6.0g Protein, 19.0g Fat, 200 Calories

Chocolate Mousse

Servings: 4 | Cooking Time: 0 Minutes

Ingredients:

- 1 large, ripe avocado
- 1/4 cup sweetened almond milk
- 1 tbsp coconut oil
- 1/4 cup cocoa or cacao powder
- 1 tsp vanilla extract

Directions:

1. In a food processor, process all ingredients until smooth and creamy.
2. Transfer to a lidded container and chill for at least 4 hours.
3. Serve and enjoy.

Nutrition Info:

- Per Servings 6.9g Carbs, 1.2g Protein, 11.0g Fat, 125 Calories

Asian Glazed Meatballs

Servings: 4 | Cooking Time: 35 Minutes

Ingredients:

- 1-pound frozen meatballs, thawed to room temperature
- ½ cup hoisin sauce
- 1 tablespoon apricot jam
- 2 tablespoons soy sauce
- ½ teaspoon sesame oil
- 5 tbsp MCT oil or coconut oil
- 2 tbsp water

Directions:

1. Place a heavy-bottomed pot on medium-high fire and heat coconut oil.
2. Sauté meatballs until lightly browned, around 10 minutes.
3. Stir in remaining ingredients and mix well.
4. Cover and cook for 25 minutes on low fire, mixing now and then.
5. Serve and enjoy.

Nutrition Info:

- Per Servings 6.5g Carbs, 16.3g Protein, 51.6g Fat, 536 Calories

Bacon-flavored Kale Chips

Servings: 6 | Cooking Time: 25 Minutes

Ingredients:
- 2 tbsp butter
- ¼ cup bacon grease
- 1-lb kale, around 1 bunch
- 1 to 2 tsp salt

Directions:
1. Remove the rib from kale leaves and tear it into 2-inch pieces.
2. Clean the kale leaves thoroughly and dry them inside a salad spinner.
3. In a skillet, add the butter to the bacon grease and warm the two fats under low heat. Add salt and stir constantly.
4. Set aside and let it cool.
5. Put the dried kale in a Ziploc back and add the cool liquid bacon grease and butter mixture.
6. Seal the Ziploc back and gently shake the kale leaves with the butter mixture. The leaves should have this shiny consistency, which means that they are coated evenly with the fat.
7. Pour the kale leaves on a cookie sheet and sprinkle more salt if necessary.
8. Bake for 25 minutes inside a preheated 350oF oven or until the leaves start to turn brown as well as crispy.

Nutrition Info:
- Per Servings 6.6g Carbs, 3.3g Protein, 13.1g Fat, 148 Calories

Shrimp Fra Diavolo

Servings: 3 | Cooking Time: 5 Minutes

Ingredients:
- 3 tablespoons butter
- 1 onion, diced
- 5 cloves of garlic, minced
- 1 teaspoon red pepper flakes
- ¼ pound shrimps, shelled
- 2 tablespoons olive oil
- Salt and pepper to taste

Directions:
1. Heat the butter and the olive oil in a skillet and sauté the onion and garlic until fragrant.
2. Stir in the red pepper flakes and shrimps. Season with salt and pepper to taste.
3. Stir for 3 minutes.
4. Serve and enjoy.

Nutrition Info:
- Per Servings 4.5g Carbs, 21.0g Protein, 32.1g Fat, 388 Calories

Cheddar Cheese Chips

Servings: 4 | Cooking Time: 8 Minutes

Ingredients:

- 8 oz cheddar cheese or provolone cheese or Edam cheese, in slices
- ½ tsp paprika powder

Directions:

1. Line baking sheet with foil and preheat oven to 400F.
2. Place cheese slices on a baking sheet and sprinkle the paprika powder on top.
3. Pop in the oven and bake for 8 to 10 minutes.
4. Pay an attention when the timer reaches 6 to 7 minutes as a burnt cheese tastes bitter.
5. Serve and enjoy.

Nutrition Info:

- Per Servings 2.0g Carbs, 13.0g Protein, 19.0g Fat, 228 Calories

French Fried Butternut Squash

Servings: 6 | Cooking Time: 20 Minutes

Ingredients:

- 1 medium butternut squash
- 1 tablespoon chopped fresh thyme
- 1 tablespoon chopped fresh rosemary
- 4 tablespoons olive oil
- 1/2 teaspoon salt
- Cooking spray

Directions:

1. Heat oven to 425oF. Lightly coat a baking sheet with cooking spray.
2. Peel skin from butternut squash and cut into even sticks, about 1/2-inch-wide and 3 inches long.
3. In a medium bowl, combine the squash, oil, thyme, rosemary, and salt; mix until the squash is evenly coated.
4. Spread onto the baking sheet and roast for 10 minutes.
5. Remove the baking sheet from the oven and shake to loosen the squash.
6. Return to oven and continue to roast for 10 minutes or until golden brown.
7. Serve and enjoy.

Nutrition Info:

- Per Servings 1g Carbs, 1g Protein, 9g Fat, 86 Calories

Baba Ganoush Eggplant Dip

Servings: 4 | Cooking Time: 80 Minutes

Ingredients:

- 1 head of garlic, unpeeled
- 1 large eggplant, cut in half lengthwise
- 5 tablespoons olive oil
- Lemon juice to taste
- 2 minced garlic cloves
- What you'll need from the store cupboard:
- Pepper and salt to taste

Directions:

1. With the rack in the middle position, preheat oven to 350°F.
2. Line a baking sheet with parchment paper. Place the eggplant cut side down on the baking sheet.
3. Roast until the flesh is very tender and pulls away easily from the skin, about 1 hour depending on the eggplant's size. Let it cool.
4. Meanwhile, cut the tips off the garlic cloves. Place the cloves in a square of aluminum foil. Fold up the edges of the foil and crimp together to form a tightly sealed packet. Roast alongside the eggplant until tender, about 20 minutes. Let cool.
5. Mash the cloves by pressing with a fork.
6. With a spoon, scoop the flesh from the eggplant and place it in the bowl of a food processor. Add the mashed garlic, oil and lemon juice. Process until smooth. Season with pepper.

Nutrition Info:

- Per Servings 10.2g Carbs, 1.6g Protein, 17.8g Fat, 192 Calories

Turkey Pastrami & Mascarpone Cheese Pinwheels

Servings: 4 | Cooking Time: 40 Minutes

Ingredients:

- Cooking spray
- 8 oz mascarpone cheese
- 10 oz turkey pastrami, sliced
- 10 canned pepperoncini peppers, sliced and drained

Directions:

1. Lay a 12 x 12 plastic wrap on a flat surface and arrange the pastrami all over slightly overlapping each other. Spread the cheese on top of the salami layers and arrange the pepperoncini on top.
2. Hold two opposite ends of the plastic wrap and roll the pastrami. Twist both ends to tighten and refrigerate for 2 hours. Unwrap the salami roll and slice into 2-inch pinwheels. Serve.

Nutrition Info:

- Per Servings 0g Carbs, 13g Protein, 24g Fat, 266 Calories

Mozzarella & Prosciutto Wraps

Servings: 6 | Cooking Time: 15 Minutes

Ingredients:

- 6 thin prosciutto slices
- 18 basil leaves
- 18 mozzarella ciliegine

Directions:

1. Cut the prosciutto slices into three strips. Place basil leaves at the end of each strip. Top with mozzarella. Wrap the mozzarella in prosciutto. Secure with toothpicks.

Nutrition Info:

- Per Servings 0.1g Carbs, 13g Protein, 12g Fat, 163 Calories

Mascarpone Snapped Amaretti Biscuits

Servings: 6 | Cooking Time: 25 Minutes

Ingredients:

- 6 egg whites
- 1 egg yolk, beaten
- 1 tsp vanilla bean paste
- 8 oz swerve confectioner's sugar
- A pinch of salt
- ¼ cup ground fragrant almonds
- 1 lemon juice
- 7 tbsp sugar-free amaretto liquor
- ¼ cup mascarpone cheese
- ¼ cup butter, room temperature
- ¾ cup swerve confectioner's sugar, for topping

Directions:

1. Preheat an oven to 300ºF and line a baking sheet with parchment paper. Set aside.
2. In a bowl, beat eggs whites, salt, and vanilla paste with the hand mixer while you gradually spoon in 8 oz of swerve confectioner's sugar until a stiff mixture. Add ground almonds and fold in the egg yolk, lemon juice, and amaretto liquor. Spoon the mixture into the piping bag and press out 40 to 50 mounds on the baking sheet.
3. Bake the biscuits for 15 minutes by which time they should be golden brown. Whisk the mascarpone cheese, butter, and swerve confectioner's sugar with the cleaned electric mixer; set aside.
4. When the biscuits are ready, transfer them into a serving bowl and let cool. Spread a scoop of mascarpone cream onto one biscuit and snap with another biscuit. Sift some swerve confectioner's sugar on top of them and serve.

Nutrition Info:

- Per Servings 3g Carbs, 9g Protein, 13g Fat, 165 Calories

Walnut Butter On Cracker

Servings: 1 | Cooking Time: 0 Minutes

Ingredients:

- 1 tablespoon walnut butter
- 2 pieces Mary's gone crackers

Directions:

1. Spread ½ tablespoon of walnut butter per cracker and enjoy.

Nutrition Info:

- Per Servings 4.0g Carbs, 1.0g Protein, 14.0g Fat, 134 Calories

Stuffed Jalapeno

Servings: 4 | Cooking Time: 20 Minutes

Ingredients:

- 12 jalapeno peppers, halved lengthwise and seeded
- 2-oz cream cheese softened
- 2-oz shredded cheddar cheese
- ¼ cup almond meal
- Salt and pepper to taste

Directions:

1. Spray a cookie sheet with cooking spray and preheat oven to 400oF.
2. Equally fill each jalapeno with cheddar cheese, cream cheese, and sprinkle almond meal on top. Place on a prepped baking sheet.
3. Pop in oven and bake for 20 minutes.
4. Serve and enjoy.

Nutrition Info:

- Per Servings 7.7g Carbs, 5.9g Protein, 13.2g Fat, 187 Calories

Chapter 3 Vegan, Vegetable & Meat-less Recipes

Chapter 3 Vegan, Vegetable & Meatless Recipes

Cheesy Cauliflower Falafel

Servings: 4 | Cooking Time: 15 Minutes

Ingredients:

- 1 head cauliflower, cut into florets
- ⅓ cup silvered ground almonds
- ½ tsp mixed spice
- Salt and chili pepper to taste
- 3 tbsp coconut flour
- 3 fresh eggs
- 4 tbsp ghee

Directions:

1. Blend the cauli florets in a food processor until a grain meal consistency is formed. Pour the puree in a bowl, add the ground almonds, mixed spice, salt, chili pepper, and coconut flour, and mix until evenly combined.
2. Beat the eggs in a bowl until creamy in color and mix with the cauli mixture. Shape ¼ cup each into patties and set aside.
3. Melt ghee in a frying pan over medium heat and fry the patties for 5 minutes on each side to be firm and browned. Remove onto a wire rack to cool, share into serving plates, and top with tahini sauce.

Nutrition Info:

- Per Servings 2g Carbs, 8g Protein, 26g Fat, 315 Calories

Creamy Vegetable Stew

Servings: 4 | Cooking Time: 32 Minutes

Ingredients:

- 2 tbsp ghee
- 1 tbsp onion garlic puree
- 4 medium carrots, peeled and chopped
- 1 large head cauliflower, cut into florets
- 2 cups green beans, halved
- Salt and black pepper to taste
- 1 cup water
- 1 ½ cups heavy cream

Directions:

1. Melt ghee in a saucepan over medium heat and sauté onion-garlic puree to be fragrant, 2 minutes.
2. Stir in carrots, cauliflower, and green beans, salt, and pepper, add the water, stir again, and cook the vegetables on low heat for 25 minutes to soften. Mix in the heavy cream to be incorporated, turn the heat off, and adjust the taste with salt and pepper. Serve the stew with almond flour bread.

Nutrition Info:

- Per Servings 6g Carbs, 8g Protein, 26.4g Fat, 310 Calories

Creamy Kale And Mushrooms

Servings: 3 | Cooking Time: 15 Minutes

Ingredients:

- 3 cloves of garlic, minced
- 1 onion, chopped
- 1 bunch kale, stems removed and leaves chopped
- 3 white button mushrooms, chopped
- 1 cup heavy cream
- 5 tablespoons oil
- Salt and pepper to taste

Directions:

1. Heat oil in a pot.
2. Sauté the garlic and onion until fragrant for 2 minutes.
3. Stir in mushrooms. Season with pepper and salt. Cook for 8 minutes.
4. Stir in kale and coconut milk. Simmer for 5 minutes.
5. Adjust seasoning to taste.

Nutrition Info:

- Per Servings 7.9g Carbs, 6.0g Protein, 35.5g Fat, 365 Calories

Butternut Squash And Cauliflower Stew

Servings: 4 | Cooking Time:10 Minutes

Ingredients:

- 3 cloves of garlic, minced
- 1 cup cauliflower florets
- 1 ½ cups butternut squash, cubed
- 2 ½ cups heavy cream
- Pepper and salt to taste
- 3 tbsp coconut oil

Directions:

1. Heat the oil in a pan and saute the garlic until fragrant.
2. Stir in the rest of the ingredients and season with salt and pepper to taste.
3. Close the lid and bring to a boil for 10 minutes.
4. Serve and enjoy.

Nutrition Info:

- Per Servings 10g Carbs, 2g Protein, 38.1g Fat, 385 Calories

Tofu Sesame Skewers With Warm Kale Salad

Servings: 4 | Cooking Time: 2 Hours 40 Minutes

Ingredients:

- 14 oz Firm tofu
- 4 tsp sesame oil
- 1 lemon, juiced
- 5 tbsp sugar-free soy sauce
- 3 tsp garlic powder
- 4 tbsp coconut flour
- ½ cup sesame seeds
- Warm Kale Salad:

- 4 cups chopped kale
- 2 tsp + 2 tsp olive oil
- 1 white onion, thinly sliced
- 3 cloves garlic, minced
- 1 cup sliced white mushrooms
- 1 tsp chopped rosemary
- Salt and black pepper to season
- 1 tbsp balsamic vinegar

Directions:

1. In a bowl, mix sesame oil, lemon juice, soy sauce, garlic powder, and coconut flour. Wrap the tofu in a paper towel, squeeze out as much liquid from it, and cut it into strips. Stick on the skewers, height wise. Place onto a plate, pour the soy sauce mixture over, and turn in the sauce to be adequately coated. Cover the dish with cling film and marinate in the fridge for 2 hours.

2. Heat the griddle pan over high heat. Pour the sesame seeds in a plate and roll the tofu skewers in the seeds for a generous coat. Grill the tofu in the griddle pan to be golden brown on both sides, about 12 minutes in total.

3. Heat 2 tablespoons of olive oil in a skillet over medium heat and sauté onion to begin browning for 10 minutes with continuous stirring. Add the remaining olive oil and mushrooms. Continue cooking for 10 minutes. Add garlic, rosemary, salt, pepper, and balsamic vinegar. Cook for 1 minute.

4. Put the kale in a salad bowl; when the onion mixture is ready, pour it on the kale and toss well. Serve the tofu skewers with the warm kale salad and a peanut butter dipping sauce.

Nutrition Info:

- Per Servings 6.1g Carbs, 5.6g Protein, 12.9g Fat, 263 Calories

Creamy Cucumber Avocado Soup

Servings: 4 | Cooking Time: 15 Minutes

Ingredients:

- 4 large cucumbers, seeded, chopped
- 1 large avocado, peeled and pitted
- Salt and black pepper to taste
- 2 cups water
- 1 tbsp cilantro, chopped
- 3 tbsp olive oil
- 2 limes, juiced
- 2 tsp minced garlic
- 2 tomatoes, evenly chopped
- 1 chopped avocado for garnish

Directions:

1. Pour the cucumbers, avocado halves, salt, pepper, olive oil, lime juice, cilantro, water, and garlic in the food processor. Puree the ingredients for 2 minutes or until smooth.

2. Pour the mixture in a bowl and top with avocado and tomatoes. Serve chilled with zero-carb bread.

Nutrition Info:

- Per Servings 4.1g Carbs, 3.7g Protein, 7.4g Fat, 170 Calories

Keto Enchilada Bake

Servings: 6 | Cooking Time: 20 Minutes

Ingredients:

- 1 package House Foods Organic Extra Firm Tofu
- 1 cup roma tomatoes, chopped
- 1 cup shredded cheddar cheese
- 1 small avocado, pitted and sliced
- ½ cup sour cream
- 5 tablespoons olive oil
- Salt and pepper to taste

Directions:

1. Preheat oven to 350F.
2. Cut tofu into small cubes and sauté with oil and seasoning. Set aside and reserve the oil.
3. Place the tofu in the bottom of a casserole dish.
4. Mix the reserved oil and tomatoes and pour over the tofu.
5. Sprinkle with cheese on top.
6. Bake for 20 minutes.
7. Top with avocado and sour cream toppings.
8. Serve and enjoy.

Nutrition Info:

- Per Servings 6g Carbs, 38g Protein, 40g Fat, 568 Calories

Vegan Mushroom Pizza

Servings: 4 | Cooking Time: 35 Minutes

Ingredients:

- 2 tsp ghee
- 1 cup chopped button mushrooms
- ½ cup sliced mixed colored bell peppers
- Pink salt and black pepper to taste
- 1 almond flour pizza bread
- 1 cup tomato sauce
- 1 tsp vegan Parmesan cheese
- Vegan Parmesan cheese for garnish

Directions:

1. Melt ghee in a skillet over medium heat, sauté the mushrooms and bell peppers for 10 minutes to soften. Season with salt and black pepper. Turn the heat off.
2. Put the pizza bread on a pizza pan, spread the tomato sauce all over the top and scatter vegetables evenly on top. Season with a little more salt and sprinkle with parmesan cheese.
3. Bake for 20 minutes until the vegetables are soft and the cheese has melted and is bubbly. Garnish with extra parmesan cheese. Slice pizza and serve with chilled berry juice.

Nutrition Info:

- Per Servings 8g Carbs, 15g Protein, 20g Fat, 295 Calories

Zesty Frittata With Roasted Chilies

Servings: 4 | Cooking Time: 17 Minutes

Ingredients:

- 2 large green bell peppers, seeded, chopped
- 4 red and yellow chilies, roasted
- 2 tbsp red wine vinegar
- 1 knob butter, melted
- 8 sprigs parsley, chopped
- 8 eggs, cracked into a bowl
- 4 tbsp olive oil
- ½ cup grated Parmesan
- ¼ cup crumbled goat cheese
- 4 cloves garlic, minced
- 1 cup loosely filled salad leaves

Directions:

1. Preheat the oven to 400°F. With a knife, seed the chilies, cut into long strips, and pour into a bowl.
2. Mix in the vinegar, butter, half of the parsley, half of the olive oil, and garlic; set aside. In another bowl, whisk the eggs with salt, pepper, bell peppers, parmesan, and the remaining parsley.
3. Now, heat the remaining oil in the cast iron over medium heat and pour the egg mixture along with half of the goat cheese. Let cook for 3 minutes and when it is near done, sprinkle the remaining goat cheese on it, and transfer the cast iron to the oven.
4. Bake the frittata for 4 more minutes, remove and drizzle with the chili oil. Garnish the frittata with salad greens and serve for lunch.

Nutrition Info:

- Per Servings 2.3g Carbs, 6.4g Protein, 10.3g Fat, 153 Calories

Wild Mushroom And Asparagus Stew

Servings: 4 | Cooking Time: 25 Minutes

Ingredients:

- 2 tbsp olive oil
- 1 cup onions, chopped
- 2 garlic cloves, pressed
- ½ cup celery, chopped
- 2 carrots, chopped
- 1 cup wild mushrooms, sliced
- 2 tbsp dry white wine
- 2 rosemary sprigs, chopped
- 1 thyme sprig, chopped
- 4 cups vegetable stock
- ½ tsp chili pepper
- 1 tsp smoked paprika
- 2 tomatoes, chopped
- 1 tbsp flax seed meal

Directions:

1. Set a stockpot over medium heat and warm oil. Add in onions and cook until tender.
2. Place in carrots, celery, and garlic and cook until soft for 4 more minutes. Add in mushrooms; cook the mixture the liquid is lost; set the vegetables aside. Stir in wine to deglaze the stockpot's bottom. Place in thyme and rosemary. Pour in tomatoes, vegetable stock, paprika, and chili pepper; add in reserved vegetables and allow to boil.
3. On low heat, allow the mixture to simmer for 15 minutes while covered. Stir in flax seed meal to thicken the stew. Plate into individual bowls and serve.

Nutrition Info:

- Per Servings 9.5g Carbs, 2.1g Protein, 7.3g Fat, 114 Calories

Roasted Brussels Sprouts With Sunflower Seeds

Servings: 6 | Cooking Time: 45 Minutes

Ingredients:

- Nonstick cooking spray
- 3 pounds brussels sprouts, halved
- ¼ cup olive oil
- Salt and ground black pepper, to taste
- 1 tsp sunflower seeds
- 2 tbsp fresh chives, chopped

Directions:

1. Set oven to 390ºF. Apply a nonstick cooking spray to a rimmed baking sheet. Arrange sprout halves on the baking sheet. Shake in black pepper, salt, sunflower seeds, and olive oil.
2. Roast for 40 minutes, until the cabbage becomes soft. Apply a garnish of fresh chopped chives.

Nutrition Info:

- Per Servings 8g Carbs, 2.1g Protein, 17g Fat, 186 Calories

Kale Cheese Waffles

Servings: 4 | Cooking Time: 45 Minutes

Ingredients:

- 2 green onions
- 1 tbsp olive oil
- 2 eggs
- ⅓ cup Parmesan cheese
- 1 cup kale, chopped
- 1 cup mozzarella cheese
- ½ cauliflower head
- 1 tsp garlic powder
- 1 tbsp sesame seeds
- 2 tsp chopped thyme

Directions:

1. Place the chopped cauliflower in the food processor and process until rice is formed. Add kale, spring onions, and thyme to the food processor. Pulse until smooth. Transfer to a bowl. Stir in the rest of the ingredients and mix to combine.
2. Heat waffle iron and spread in the mixture, evenly. Cook following the manufacturer's instructions.

Nutrition Info:

- Per Servings 3.6g Carbs, 16g Protein, 20.2g Fat, 283 Calories

Onion & Nuts Stuffed Mushrooms

Servings: 4 | Cooking Time: 30 Minutes

Ingredients:

- 1 tbsp sesame oil
- 1 onion, chopped
- 1 garlic clove, minced
- 1 pound mushrooms, stems removed
- Salt and black pepper, to taste
- ¼ cup raw pine nuts
- 2 tbsp parsley, chopped

Directions:

1. Set oven to 360ºF. Use a nonstick cooking spray to grease a large baking sheet. Into a frying pan, add sesame oil and warm. Place in garlic and onion and cook until soft.
2. Chop the mushroom stems and cook until tender. Turn off the heat, sprinkle with pepper and salt; add in pine nuts. Take the nut/mushroom mixture and stuff them to the mushroom caps and set on the baking sheet.
3. Bake the stuffed mushrooms for 30 minutes and remove to a wire rack to cool slightly. Add fresh parsley for garnish and serve.

Nutrition Info:

- Per Servings 7.4g Carbs, 4.8g Protein, 11.2g Fat, 139 Calories

Sriracha Tofu With Yogurt Sauce

Servings: 4 | Cooking Time: 40 Minutes

Ingredients:

- 12 ounces tofu, pressed and sliced
- 1 cup green onions, chopped
- 1 garlic clove, minced
- 2 tbsp vinegar
- 1 tbsp sriracha sauce
- 2 tbsp olive oil
- For Yogurt Sauce
- 2 cloves garlic, pressed
- 2 tbsp fresh lemon juice
- Sea salt and black pepper, to taste
- 1 tsp fresh dill weed
- 1 cup Greek yogurt
- 1 cucumber, shredded

Directions:

1. Put tofu slices, garlic, Sriracha sauce, vinegar, and scallions in a bowl; allow to settle for approximately 30 minutes. Set oven to medium-high heat and add oil in a nonstick skillet to warm. Cook tofu for 5 minutes until golden brown.
2. For the preparation of sauce, use a bowl to mix garlic, salt, yogurt, black pepper, lemon juice, and dill. Add in shredded cucumber as you stir to combine well. Put the yogurt sauce in your fridge until ready to serve. Serve the tofu in serving plates with a dollop of yogurt sauce.

Nutrition Info:

- Per Servings 8.1g Carbs, 17.5g Protein, 25.9g Fat, 351 Calories

Tomato Stuffed Avocado

Servings: 4 | Cooking Time: 10 Minutes

Ingredients:

- 2 avocados, peeled and pitted
- 1 tomato, chopped
- ¼ cup walnuts, ground
- 2 carrots, chopped
- 1 garlic clove
- 1 tsp lemon juice
- 1 tbsp soy sauce
- Salt and black pepper, to taste

Directions:

1. Using a mixing bowl, mix soy sauce, carrots, avocado pulp, lemon juice, walnuts, and garlic.
2. Add pepper and salt. Plate the mixture into the avocado halves. Scatter walnuts over to serve.

Nutrition Info:

- Per Servings 5.5g Carbs, 3.5g Protein, 24.8g Fat, 263 Calories

Creamy Artichoke And Spinach

Servings: 4 | Cooking Time: 15 Minutes

Ingredients:

- 5 tablespoons olive oil
- 1 can water-packed artichoke hearts quartered
- 1 package frozen spinach
- 1 cup shredded part-skim mozzarella cheese, divided
- 1/4 cup grated Parmesan cheese
- 1/2 teaspoon salt
- 1/4 teaspoon pepper

Directions:

1. Heat oil in a pan over medium flame. Add artichoke hearts and season with salt and pepper to taste. Cook for 5 minutes. Stir in the spinach until wilted.
2. Place in a bowl and stir in mozzarella cheese, Parmesan cheese, salt, and pepper. Toss to combine.
3. Transfer to a greased 2-qt. Broiler-safe baking dish; sprinkle with remaining mozzarella cheese. Broil 4-6 in. from heat 2-3 minutes or until cheese is melted.

Nutrition Info:

- Per Servings 7.3g Carbs, 11.5g Protein, 23.9g Fat, 283 Calories

Fall Roasted Vegetables

Servings: 4 | Cooking Time: 45 Minutes

Ingredients:

- 1 red bell pepper, sliced
- 1 green bell pepper, sliced
- 1 orange bell pepper, sliced
- ½ head broccoli, cut into florets
- 2 zucchinis, sliced
- 2 leeks, chopped
- 4 garlic cloves, halved
- 2 thyme sprigs, chopped
- 1 tsp dried sage, crushed
- 4 tbsp olive oil
- 2 tbsp vinegar
- 4 tbsp tomato puree
- Sea salt and cayenne pepper, to taste

Directions:

1. Set oven to 425 °F. Apply nonstick cooking spray to a rimmed baking sheet. Mix all vegetables with oil, seasonings, and vinegar; shake well. Roast for 40 minutes, flipping once halfway through.

Nutrition Info:

- Per Servings 8.2g Carbs, 2.1g Protein, 14.3g Fat, 165 Calories

Brussels Sprouts With Tofu

Servings: 4 | Cooking Time: 20 Minutes

Ingredients:

- 2 tbsp olive oil
- 2 garlic cloves, minced
- ½ cup onion, chopped
- 10 ounces tofu, crumbled
- 2 tbsp water
- 2 tbsp soy sauce
- 1 tbsp tomato puree
- ½ pound Brussels sprouts, quartered
- Sea salt and black pepper, to taste

Directions:

1. Set a saucepan over medium-high heat and warm the oil. Add onion and garlic and cook until tender. Place in the soy sauce, water, and tofu. Cook for 5 minutes until the tofu starts to brown.
2. Add in brussels sprouts; apply pepper and salt for seasoning; reduce heat to low and cook for 13 minutes while stirring frequently. Serve while warm.

Nutrition Info:

- Per Servings 12.1g Carbs, 10.5g Protein, 11.7g Fat, 179 Calories

Herb Butter With Parsley

Servings: 1 | Cooking Time: 0 Minutes

Ingredients:

- 5 oz. butter, at room temperature
- 1 garlic clove, pressed
- ½ tbsp garlic powder
- 4 tbsp fresh parsley, finely chopped
- 1 tsp lemon juice
- ½ tsp salt

Directions:

1. In a bowl, stir all ingredients until completely combined. Set aside for 15 minutes or refrigerate it before serving.

Nutrition Info:

- Per Servings 1g Carbs, 1g Protein, 28g Fat, 258 Calories

Garlic Lemon Mushrooms

Servings: 4 | Cooking Time: 20 Minutes

Ingredients:

- 1/4 cup lemon juice
- 3 tablespoons minced fresh parsley
- 3 garlic cloves, minced
- 1-pound large fresh mushrooms
- 4 tablespoons olive oil
- Pepper to taste

Directions:

1. For the dressing, whisk together the first 5 ingredients. Toss mushrooms with 2 tablespoons dressing.
2. Grill mushrooms, covered, over medium-high heat until tender, 5-7 minutes per side. Toss with remaining dressing before serving.

Nutrition Info:

- Per Servings 6.8g Carbs, 4g Protein, 14g Fat, 160 Calories

Cauliflower Mac And Cheese

Servings: 7 | Cooking Time: 45 Minutes

Ingredients:

- 1 cauliflower head, riced
- 1 ½ cups shredded cheese
- 2 tsp paprika
- ¾ tsp rosemary
- 2 tsp turmeric
- 3 eggs
- Olive oil, for frying

Directions:

1. Microwave the cauliflower for 5 minutes. Place it in cheesecloth and squeeze the extra juices out. Place the cauliflower in a bowl. Stir in the rest of the ingredients.
2. Heat the oil in a deep pan until it reaches 360ºF. Add the 'mac and cheese' and fry until golden and crispy. Drain on paper towels before serving.

Nutrition Info:

- Per Servings 2g Carbs, 8.6g Protein, 12g Fat, 160 Calories

Spaghetti Squash With Eggplant & Parmesan

Servings: 4 | Cooking Time: 15 Minutes

Ingredients:

- 1 tbsp butter
- 1 cup cherry tomatoes
- 2 tbsp parsley
- 1 eggplant, cubed
- ¼ cup Parmesan cheese
- 3 tbsp scallions, chopped
- 1 cup snap peas
- 1 tsp lemon zest
- 2 cups cooked spaghetti squash

Directions:

1. Melt the butter in a saucepan and cook eggplant for 5 minutes until tender. Add the tomatoes and peas, and cook for 5 more minutes. Stir in parsley, zest, and scallions, and remove the pan from heat. Stir in spaghetti squash and parmesan.

Nutrition Info:

- Per Servings 6.8g Carbs, 6.9g Protein, 8.2g Fat, 139 Calories

Zucchini Lasagna With Ricotta And Spinach

Servings: 4 | Cooking Time: 50 Minutes

Ingredients:

- Cooking spray
- 2 zucchinis, sliced
- Salt and black pepper to taste
- 2 cups ricotta cheese
- 2 cups shredded mozzarella cheese
- 3 cups tomato sauce
- 1 cup packed baby spinach

Directions:

1. Preheat oven to 370ºF and grease a baking dish with cooking spray.
2. Put the zucchini slices in a colander and sprinkle with salt. Let sit and drain liquid for 5 minutes and pat dry with paper towels. Mix the ricotta, mozzarella, salt, and pepper to evenly combine and spread ¼ cup of the mixture in the bottom of the baking dish.
3. Layer ⅓ of the zucchini slices on top spread 1 cup of tomato sauce over, and scatter a ⅓ cup of spinach on top. Repeat the layering process two more times to exhaust the ingredients while making sure to layer with the last ¼ cup of cheese mixture finally.
4. Grease one end of foil with cooking spray and cover the baking dish with the foil. Bake for 35 minutes, remove foil, and bake further for 5 to 10 minutes or until the cheese has a nice golden brown color. Remove the dish, sit for 5 minutes, make slices of the lasagna, and serve warm.

Nutrition Info:

- Per Servings 2g Carbs, 7g Protein, 39g Fat, 390 Calories

Chard Swiss Dip

Servings: 6 | Cooking Time: 25 Minutes

Ingredients:

- 2 cups Swiss chard
- 1 cup tofu, pressed, drained, crumbled
- ½ cup almond milk
- 2 tsp nutritional yeast
- 2 garlic cloves, minced
- 2 tbsp olive oil
- Salt and pepper to taste
- ½ tsp paprika
- ½ tsp chopped fresh mint leaves

Directions:

1. Set oven to 400ºF. Spray a nonstick cooking spray on a casserole pan. Boil Swiss chard until wilted. Using a blender, puree the remaining ingredients. Season with salt and pepper. Stir in the Swiss chard to get a homogeneous mixture. Bake for 13 minutes. Serve alongside baked vegetables.

Nutrition Info:

- Per Servings 7.9g Carbs, 2.9g Protein, 7.3g Fat, 105 Calories

Portobello Mushroom Burgers

Servings: 4 | Cooking Time: 15 Minutes

Ingredients:

- 4 low carb buns
- 4 portobello mushroom caps
- 1 clove garlic, minced
- ½ tsp salt
- 2 tbsp olive oil
- ½ cup sliced roasted red peppers
- 2 medium tomatoes, chopped
- ¼ cup crumbled feta cheese
- 1 tbsp red wine vinegar
- 2 tbsp pitted kalamata olives, chopped
- ½ tsp dried oregano
- 2 cups baby salad greens

Directions:

1. Heat the grill pan over medium-high heat and while it heats, crush the garlic with salt in a bowl using the back of a spoon. Stir in 1 tablespoon of oil and brush the mushrooms and each inner side of the buns with the mixture.
2. Place the mushrooms in the heated pan and grill them on both sides for 8 minutes until tender.
3. Also, toast the buns in the pan until they are crisp, about 2 minutes. Set aside.
4. In a bowl, mix the red peppers, tomatoes, olives, feta cheese, vinegar, oregano, baby salad greens, and remaining oil; toss them. Assemble the burger: in a slice of bun, add a mushroom cap, a scoop of vegetables, and another slice of bread. Serve with cheese dip.

Nutrition Info:

- Per Servings 3g Carbs, 16g Protein, 8g Fat, 190 Calories

Chapter 4 Poultry Recipes

Chapter 4 Poultry Recipes

Stir Fried Broccoli 'n Chicken

Servings: 5 | Cooking Time: 20 Minutes

Ingredients:

- 1 tbsp. coconut oil
- 3 cloves of garlic, minced
- 1 ½ lb. chicken breasts, cut into strips
- ¼ cup coconut aminos
- 1 head broccoli, cut into florets
- Pepper to taste

Directions:

1. On medium fire, heat a saucepan for 2 minutes. Add oil to the pan and swirl to coat bottom and sides. Heat oil for a minute.
2. Add garlic and sauté for a minute. Stir in chicken and stir fry for 5 minutes.
3. Add remaining ingredients. Season generously with pepper.
4. Increase fire to high and stir fry for 3 minutes.
5. Lower fire to low, cover, and cook for 5 minutes.
6. Serve and enjoy.

Nutrition Info:

- Per Servings 1.8g Carbs, 28.6g Protein, 15.4g Fat, 263 Calories

Oregano & Chili Flattened Chicken

Servings: 6 | Cooking Time: 5 Minutes

Ingredients:

- 6 chicken breasts
- 4 cloves garlic, minced
- ½ cup oregano leaves, chopped
- ½ cup lemon juice
- 2/3 cup olive oil
- ¼ cup erythritol
- Salt and black pepper to taste
- 3 small chilies, minced

Directions:

1. Preheat a grill to 350ºF.
2. In a bowl, mix the garlic, oregano, lemon Juice, olive oil, and erythritol. Set aside.
3. While the spices incorporate in flavor, cover the chicken with plastic wraps, and use the rolling pin to pound to ½ -inch thickness. Remove the wrap afterward, and brush the mixture on the chicken on both sides. Place on the grill, cover the lid and cook for 15 minutes.
4. Then, baste the chicken with more of the spice mixture, and continue cooking for 15 more minutes.

Nutrition Info:

- Per Servings 3g Carbs, 26g Protein, 9g Fat, 265 Calories

Broccoli Chicken Stew

Servings: 4 | Cooking Time: 30 Minutes

Ingredients:

- 1 package frozen chopped broccoli
- 1 cup shredded sharp cheddar cheese
- ½ cup sour cream
- ¾ cup Campbell's broccoli cheese soup
- 4 boneless skinless chicken breasts, thawed
- ½ cup water

Directions:

1. Add all ingredients, except for broccoli in a pot on high fire and bring to a boil.
2. Once boiling, lower fire to a simmer and cook for 20 minutes, stirring frequently.
3. Adjust seasoning to taste. Add broccoli and continue cooking and stirring for another 5 minutes.
4. Serve and enjoy.

Nutrition Info:

- Per Servings 9.7g Carbs, 63.9g Protein, 22.1g Fat, 511 Calories

Easy Bbq Chicken And Cheese

Servings: 4 | Cooking Time: 40 Minutes

Ingredients:

- 1-pound chicken tenders, boneless
- ½ cup commercial BBQ sauce, keto-friendly
- 1 teaspoon liquid smoke
- 1 cup mozzarella cheese, grated
- ½ pound bacon, fried and crumbled
- Pepper and salt to taste

Directions:

1. With paper towels, dry chicken tenders. Season with pepper and salt.
2. Place chicken tenders on an oven-safe dish.
3. Whisk well BBQ sauce and liquid smoke in a bowl and pour over chicken tenders. Coat well in the sauce.
4. Bake in a preheated 400oF oven for 30 minutes.
5. Remove from oven, turnover chicken tenders, sprinkle cheese on top.
6. Return to the oven and continue baking for 10 minutes more.
7. Serve and enjoy with a sprinkle of bacon bits.

Nutrition Info:

- Per Servings 6.7g Carbs, 34.6g Protein, 31.5g Fat, 351 Calories

Zucchini Spaghetti With Turkey Bolognese Sauce

Servings: 6 | Cooking Time: 30 Minutes

Ingredients:

- 2 cups sliced mushrooms
- 2 tsp olive oil
- 1 pound ground turkey
- 3 tbsp pesto sauce
- 1 cup diced onion
- 2 cups broccoli florets
- 6 cups zucchini, spiralized

Directions:

1. Heat the oil in a skillet. Add zucchini and cook for 2-3 minutes, stirring continuously; set aside.
2. Add turkey to the skillet and cook until browned, about 7-8 minutes. Transfer to a plate. Add onion and cook until translucent, about 3 minutes. Add broccoli and mushrooms, and cook for 7 more minutes. Return the turkey to the skillet. Stir in the pesto sauce. Cover the pan, lower the heat, and simmer for 15 minutes. Stir in zucchini pasta and serve immediately.

Nutrition Info:

- Per Servings 3.8g Carbs, 19g Protein, 16g Fat, 273 Calories

Chili Lime Chicken

Servings: 5 | Cooking Time: 30 Minutes

Ingredients:

- 1 lb. chicken breasts, skin and bones removed
- Juice from 1 ½ limes, freshly squeezed
- 1 tbsp. chili powder
- 1 tsp. cumin
- 6 cloves garlic, minced
- Pepper and salt to taste
- 1 cup water
- 4 tablespoon olive oil

Directions:

1. Place all ingredients in a heavy-bottomed pot and give a good stir.
2. Place on high fire and bring it to a boil. Cover, lower fire to a simmer, and cook for 20 minutes.
3. Remove chicken and place in a bowl. Shred using two forks. Return shredded chicken to the pot.
4. Boil for 10 minutes or until sauce is rendered.
5. Serve and enjoy.

Nutrition Info:

- Per Servings 1.5g Carbs, 19.3g Protein, 19.5g Fat, 265 Calories

Chicken Wings With Thyme Chutney

Servings: 4 | Cooking Time: 45 Minutes

Ingredients:

- 12 chicken wings, cut in half
- 1 tbsp turmeric
- 1 tbsp cumin
- 3 tbsp fresh ginger, grated
- 1 tbsp cilantro, chopped
- 2 tbsp paprika
- Salt and ground black pepper, to taste
- 3 tbsp olive oil
- Juice of ½ lime
- 1 cup thyme leaves
- ¾ cup cilantro, chopped
- 1 tbsp water
- 1 jalapeño pepper

Directions:

1. Using a bowl, stir together 1 tbsp ginger, cumin, paprika, salt, 2 tbsp olive oil, pepper, turmeric, and cilantro. Place in the chicken wings pieces, toss to coat, and refrigerate for 20 minutes. Heat the grill, place in the marinated wings, cook for 25 minutes, turning from time to time, remove and set to a bowl.
2. Using a blender, combine thyme, remaining ginger, salt, jalapeno pepper, black pepper, lime juice, cilantro, remaining olive oil, and water, and blend well. Set the chicken wings on serving plate and top with the sauce.

Nutrition Info:

- Per Servings 3.5g Carbs, 22g Protein, 15g Fat, 243 Calories

Homemade Chicken Pizza Calzone

Servings: 4 | Cooking Time: 60 Minutes

Ingredients:

- 2 eggs
- 1 low carb pizza crust
- ½ cup Pecorino cheese, grated
- 1 lb chicken breasts, skinless, boneless, halved
- ½ cup sugar-free marinara sauce
- 1 tsp Italian seasoning
- 1 tsp onion powder
- 1 tsp garlic powder
- Salt and black pepper, to taste
- ¼ cup flax seed, ground
- 6 ounces provolone cheese

Directions:

1. Using a bowl, combine the Italian seasoning with onion powder, salt, Pecorino cheese, pepper, garlic powder, and flax seed. In a separate bowl, combine the eggs with pepper and salt.
2. Dip the chicken pieces in eggs, and then in seasoning mixture, lay all parts on a lined baking sheet, and bake for 25 minutes in the oven at 390° F.
3. Place the pizza crust dough on a lined baking sheet and spread half of the provolone cheese on half. Remove chicken from oven, chop it, and scatter it over the provolone cheese. Spread over the marinara sauce and top with the remaining cheese.
4. Cover with the other half of the dough and shape the pizza in a calzone. Seal the edges, set in the oven and bake for 20 minutes. Allow the calzone to cool down before slicing and enjoy.

Nutrition Info:

- Per Servings 4.6g Carbs, 28g Protein, 15g Fat, 425 Calories

Yummy Chicken Queso

Servings: 4 | Cooking Time: 25 Minutes

Ingredients:

- ½ teaspoon garlic salt
- 4-ounce can diced drained green chiles
- 10-ounce can mild rotel drained
- ¾ cup medium queso dip
- 4 boneless skinless boneless fresh or thawed chicken breasts
- 5 tablespoons olive oil
- 1 cup water

Directions:

1. Add all ingredients in a pot on high fire and bring it to a boil.
2. Once boiling, lower fire to a simmer and cook for 20 minutes. Stir frequently.
3. Adjust seasoning to taste.
4. Serve and enjoy.

Nutrition Info:

- Per Servings 7.2g Carbs, 56.6g Protein, 21.7g Fat, 500 Calories

Coconut Chicken Soup

Servings: 4 | Cooking Time: 30 Minutes

Ingredients:

- 3 tbsp butter
- 4 ounces cream cheese
- 2 chicken breasts, diced
- 4 cups chicken stock
- Salt and black pepper, to taste
- ½ cup coconut cream
- ¼ cup celery, chopped

Directions:

1. In the blender, combine stock, butter, coconut cream, salt, cream cheese, and pepper. Remove to a pot, heat over medium heat, and stir in the chicken and celery. Simmer for 15 minutes, separate into bowls, and enjoy.

Nutrition Info:

- Per Servings 5g Carbs, 31g Protein, 23g Fat, 387 Calories

Chicken Breasts With Cheddar & Pepperoni

Servings: 4 | Cooking Time: 40 Minutes

Ingredients:

- 12 oz canned tomato sauce
- 1 tbsp olive oil
- 4 chicken breast halves, skinless and boneless
- Salt and ground black pepper, to taste
- 1 tsp dried oregano
- 4 oz cheddar cheese, sliced
- 1 tsp garlic powder
- 2 oz pepperoni, sliced

Directions:

1. Preheat your oven to 390ºF. Using a bowl, combine chicken with oregano, salt, garlic, and pepper.
2. Heat a pan with the olive oil over medium-high heat, add in the chicken, cook each side for 2 minutes, and remove to a baking dish. Top with the cheddar cheese slices spread the sauce, then cover with pepperoni slices. Bake for 30 minutes. Serve warm garnished with fresh oregano if desired

Nutrition Info:

- Per Servings 4.5g Carbs, 32g Protein, 21g Fat, 387 Calories

Slow-cooked Mexican Turkey Soup

Servings: 4 | Cooking Time: 4 Hours 15 Minutes

Ingredients:

- 1 ½ lb turkey breasts, skinless, boneless, cubed
- 4 cups chicken stock
- 1 chopped onion
- 1 cup canned chunky salsa
- 8 ounces cheddar cheese, into chunks
- ¼ tsp cayenne red pepper
- 4 oz canned diced green chilies
- 1 tsp fresh cilantro, chopped

Directions:

1. In a slow cooker, combine the turkey with salsa, onion, green chilies, cayenne pepper, chicken stock, and cheese, and cook for 4 hours on high while covered. Open the slow cooker, sprinkle with fresh cilantro and ladle in bowls to serve.

Nutrition Info:

- Per Servings 6g Carbs, 38g Protein, 24g Fat, 387 Calories

Yummy Chicken Nuggets

Servings: 2 | Cooking Time: 25 Minutes

Ingredients:

- ½ cup almond flour
- 1 egg
- 2 tbsp garlic powder
- 2 chicken breasts, cubed
- Salt and black pepper, to taste
- ½ cup butter

Directions:

1. Using a bowl, combine salt, garlic powder, flour, and pepper, and stir. In a separate bowl, beat the egg. Add the chicken breast cubes in egg mixture, then in the flour mixture. Set a pan over medium-high heat and warm butter, add in the chicken nuggets, and cook for 6 minutes on each side. Remove to paper towels, drain the excess grease and serve.

Nutrition Info:

- Per Servings 4.3g Carbs, 35g Protein, 37g Fat, 417 Calories

Whole Roasted Chicken With Lemon And Rosemary

Servings: 12 | Cooking Time: 1 Hour And 40 Minutes

Ingredients:

- 1 whole chicken
- 6 cloves of garlic, minced
- 1 lemon, sliced
- 2 sprigs rosemary
- Salt and pepper to taste

Directions:

1. Place lemon peel, 1 rosemary sprig, and 2 cloves of smashed garlic in chicken cavity.
2. Place the whole chicken in a big bowl and rub all the spices onto the surface and insides of the chicken.
3. Place the chicken on a wire rack placed on top of a baking pan. Tent with foil.
4. Cook in a preheated 350oF oven for 60 minutes.
5. Remove foil and continue baking until golden brown, around 30 minutes more.
6. Let chicken rest for 10 minutes.
7. Serve and enjoy.

Nutrition Info:

- Per Servings 0.9g Carbs, 21.3g Protein, 17.2g Fat, 248 Calories

Chicken In Creamy Mushroom Sauce

Servings: 4 | Cooking Time: 36 Minutes

Ingredients:

- 1 tbsp ghee
- 4 chicken breasts, cut into chunks
- Salt and black pepper to taste
- 1 packet white onion soup mix
- 2 cups chicken broth
- 15 baby bella mushrooms, sliced
- 1 cup heavy cream
- 1 small bunch parsley, chopped

Directions:

1. Melt ghee in a saucepan over medium heat, season the chicken with salt and black pepper, and brown on all sides for 6 minutes in total. Put in a plate.
2. In a bowl, stir the onion soup mix with chicken broth and add to the saucepan. Simmer for 3 minutes and add the mushrooms and chicken. Cover and simmer for another 20 minutes.
3. Stir in heavy cream and parsley, cook on low heat for 3 minutes, and season with salt and pepper.
4. Ladle the chicken with creamy sauce and mushrooms over beds of cauli mash. Garnish with parsley.

Nutrition Info:

- Per Servings 2g Carbs, 22g Protein, 38.2g Fat, 448 Calories

Chicken And Zucchini Bake

Servings: 4 | Cooking Time: 45 Minutes

Ingredients:

- 1 zucchini, chopped
- Salt and black pepper, to taste
- 1 tsp garlic powder
- 1 tbsp avocado oil
- 2 chicken breasts, skinless, boneless, sliced
- 1 tomato, cored and chopped
- ½ tsp dried oregano
- ½ tsp dried basil
- ½ cup mozzarella cheese, shredded

Directions:

1. Apply pepper, garlic powder and salt to the chicken. Set a pan over medium heat and warm avocado oil, add in the chicken slices, cook until golden; remove to a baking dish. To the same pan add the zucchini, tomato, pepper, basil, oregano, and salt, cook for 2 minutes, and spread over chicken.
2. Bake in the oven at 330ºF for 20 minutes. Sprinkle the mozzarella over the chicken, return to the oven, and bake for 5 minutes until the cheese is melted and bubbling. Serve with green salad.

Nutrition Info:

- Per Servings 2g Carbs, 35g Protein, 11g Fat, 235 Calories

Turkey, Coconut And Kale Chili

Servings: 5 | Cooking Time: 30 Minutes

Ingredients:

- 18 ounces turkey breasts, cubed
- 1 cup kale, chopped
- 20 ounces canned diced tomatoes
- 2 tbsp coconut oil
- 2 tbsp coconut cream
- 2 garlic cloves, peeled and minced
- 2 onions, and sliced
- 1 tbsp ground coriander
- 2 tbsp fresh ginger, grated
- 1 tbsp turmeric
- 1 tbsp cumin
- Salt and ground black pepper, to taste
- 2 tbsp chili powder

Directions:

1. Set a pan over medium-high heat and warm the coconut oil, stir in the turkey and onion, and cook for 5 minutes. Place in garlic and ginger, and cook for 1 minute. Stir in the tomatoes, pepper, turmeric, coriander, salt, cumin, and chili powder. Place in the coconut cream, and cook for 10 minutes.
2. Transfer to an immersion blender alongside kale; blend well. Allow simmering, cook for 15 minutes.

Nutrition Info:

- Per Servings 4.2g Carbs, 25g Protein, 15.2g Fat, 295 Calories

Almond-crusted Chicken Breasts

Servings: 4 | Cooking Time: 60 Minutes

Ingredients:

- 4 bacon slices, cooked and crumbled
- 4 chicken breasts
- 1 tbsp water
- ½ cup olive oil
- 1 egg, whisked
- Salt and black pepper, to taste
- 1 cup asiago cheese, shredded
- ¼ tsp garlic powder
- 1 cup ground almonds

Directions:

1. Using a bowl, combine the ground almonds with pepper, salt, and garlic. Place the whisked egg in a separate bowl and combine with water. Apply a seasoning of pepper and salt to the chicken, and dip each piece into the egg, and then into almond mixture.
2. Set a pan over medium-high heat and warm oil, add in the chicken breasts, cook until are golden-brown, and remove to a baking pan. Bake in the oven at 360ºF for 20 minutes. Scatter with Asiago cheese and bacon and return to the oven. Roast for a few minutes until the cheese melts.

Nutrition Info:

- Per Servings 1g Carbs, 41g Protein, 32g Fat, 485 Calories

Spicy Chicken Kabobs

Servings: 6 | Cooking Time: 1 Hour And 20 Minutes

Ingredients:

- 2 pounds chicken breasts, cubed
- 1 tsp sesame oil
- 1 tbsp olive oil
- 1 cup red bell pepper pieces
- 2 tbsp five spice powder
- 2 tbsp granulated sweetener
- 1 tbsp fish sauce

Directions:

1. Combine the sauces and seasonings in a bowl. Add the chicken, and let marinate for 1 hour in the fridge. Preheat the grill. Take 12 skewers and thread the chicken and bell peppers. Grill for 3 minutes per side.

Nutrition Info:

- Per Servings 3.1g Carbs, 17.5g Protein, 13.5g Fat, 198 Calories

Turkey & Leek Soup

Servings: 4 | Cooking Time: 45 Minutes

Ingredients:

- 3 celery stalks, chopped
- 2 leeks, chopped
- 1 tbsp butter
- 6 cups chicken stock
- Salt and ground black pepper, to taste
- ¼ cup fresh parsley, chopped
- 3 cups zoodles
- 3 cups turkey meat, cooked and chopped

Directions:

1. Set a pot over medium-high heat, stir in leeks and celery and cook for 5 minutes. Place in the parsley, turkey meat, pepper, salt, and stock, and cook for 20 minutes. Stir in the zoodles, and cook turkey soup for 5 minutes. Serve in bowls and enjoy.

Nutrition Info:

- Per Servings 3g Carbs, 15g Protein, 11g Fat, 305 Calories

Baked Chicken Pesto

Servings: 4 | Cooking Time:20 Minutes

Ingredients:

- 2 tsp grated parmesan cheese
- 6 tbsp shredded reduced-fat mozzarella cheese
- 1 medium tomato (thinly sliced)
- 4 tsp basil pesto
- 2 boneless, skinless chicken breasts around 1-lb
- Salt and pepper to taste

Directions:

1. In cool water, wash chicken and dry using a paper towel. Create 4 thin slices of chicken breasts by slicing horizontally.
2. Preheat oven to 400oF and then line a baking sheet with parchment or foil.
3. Put into the baking sheet the slices of chicken. Season with pepper and salt. And spread at least 1 teaspoon of pesto on each chicken slice.
4. For 15 minutes, bake the chicken and ensure that the center is no longer pink. After which remove baking sheet and top chicken with parmesan cheese, mozzarella, and tomatoes.
5. Put into the oven once again and heat for another 3 to 5 minutes to melt the cheese, then ready to serve.

Nutrition Info:

- Per Servings 2.0g Carbs, 40.0g Protein, 8.0g Fat, 238 Calories

Baked Chicken With Acorn Squash And Goat's Cheese

Servings: 6 | Cooking Time: 1 Hour 15 Minutes

Ingredients:

- 6 chicken breasts, skinless and boneless
- 1 lb acorn squash, peeled and sliced
- Salt and ground black pepper, to taste
- 1 cup goat's cheese, shredded
- Cooking spray

Directions:

1. Take cooking oil and spray on a baking dish, add in chicken breasts, pepper, squash, and salt and drizzle with olive. Transfer in the oven set at 420ºF, and bake for 1 hour. Scatter goat's cheese, and bake for 15 minutes. Remove to a serving plate and enjoy.

Nutrition Info:

- Per Servings 5g Carbs, 12g Protein, 16g Fat, 235 Calories

Chicken Stew With Sun-dried Tomatoes

Servings: 4 | Cooking Time: 60 Minutes

Ingredients:

- 2 carrots, chopped
- 2 tbsp olive oil
- 2 celery stalks, chopped
- 2 cups chicken stock
- 1 shallot, chopped
- 28 oz chicken thighs, skinless, boneless
- 3 garlic cloves, peeled and minced
- ½ tsp dried rosemary
- 2 oz sun-dried tomatoes, chopped
- 1 cup spinach
- ¼ tsp dried thyme
- ½ cup heavy cream
- Salt and ground black pepper, to taste
- A pinch of xanthan gum

Directions:

1. In a pot, heat the olive oil over medium heat and add garlic, carrots, celery, and shallot; season with salt and pepper and sauté for 5-6 minutes until tender. Stir in the chicken and cook for 5 minutes.
2. Pour in the stock, tomatoes, rosemary, and thyme, and cook for 30 minutes covered. Stir in xanthan gum, cream, and spinach; cook for 5 minutes. Adjust the seasonings and separate into bowls.

Nutrition Info:

- Per Servings 6g Carbs, 23g Protein, 11g Fat, 224 Calories

Avocado Cheese Pepper Chicken

Servings: 5 | Cooking Time: 20 Minutes

Ingredients:

- ¼ tsp. cayenne pepper
- 1½ cup. cooked and shredded chicken
- 2 tbsps. cream cheese
- 2 tbsps. lemon juice
- 2 large avocados, diced
- Black pepper and salt to taste
- ¼ cup. mayonnaise
- 1 tsp. dried thyme
- ½ tsp. onion powder
- ½ tsp. garlic powder

Directions:

1. Remove the insides of your avocado halves and set them in a bowl.
2. Stir all ingredients to avocado flesh.
3. Fill avocados with chicken mix.
4. Serve and enjoy.

Nutrition Info:

- Per Servings 5g Carbs, 24g Protein, 40g Fat, 476 Calories

Greek Chicken With Capers

Servings: 4 | Cooking Time: 30 Minutes

Ingredients:

- ¼ cup olive oil
- 1 onion, chopped
- 4 chicken breasts, skinless and boneless
- 4 garlic cloves, minced
- Salt and ground black pepper, to taste
- ½ cup kalamata olives, pitted and chopped
- 1 tbsp capers
- 1 pound tomatoes, chopped
- ½ tsp red chili flakes

Directions:

1. Sprinkle pepper and salt on the chicken, and rub with half of the oil. Add the chicken to a pan set over high heat, cook for 2 minutes, flip to the other side, and cook for 2 more minutes. Set the chicken breasts in the oven at 450°F and bake for 8 minutes. Split the chicken into serving plates.

2. Set the same pan over medium heat and warm the remaining oil, place in the onion, olives, capers, garlic, and chili flakes, and cook for 1 minute. Stir in the tomatoes, pepper, and salt, and cook for 2 minutes. Sprinkle over the chicken breasts and enjoy.

Nutrition Info:

- Per Servings 2.2g Carbs, 25g Protein, 21g Fat, 387 Calories

Chapter 5 Pork, Beef & Lamb Recipes

Chapter 5 Pork, Beef & Lamb Recipes

Garlic Pork Chops

Servings: 4 | Cooking Time: 30 Minutes

Ingredients:

- 1 ½ cups chicken broth
- 1 tablespoon butter
- 2 lemons, juiced
- 4 ¾ inch boneless pork chops
- 6 cloves garlic, minced
- Salt and pepper to taste
- 1 tablespoon olive oil

Directions:

1. Heat the olive oil in a large pot on medium-high fire.
2. Season the pork with salt, pepper, and garlic powder.
3. Place the pork in the Instant Pot and brown the sides. Set aside.
4. Add the garlic and sauté for a minute. Add the lemon juice and chicken broth. Stir in the butter.
5. Add the pork chops back to the pan. Cover the lid and simmer for 20 minutes.
6. Serve and enjoy.

Nutrition Info:

- Per Servings 4.8g Carbs, 50.2g Protein, 14.0g Fat, 355 Calories

Easy Thai 5-spice Pork Stew

Servings: 9 | Cooking Time: 40 Minutes

Ingredients:

- 2 lb. pork butt, cut into chunks
- 2 tbsp. 5-spice powder
- 2 cups coconut milk, freshly squeezed
- 1 ½ tbsp sliced ginger
- 1 cup chopped cilantro
- 1 tsp oil
- Salt and pepper to taste
- ½ cup water

Directions:

1. Place a heavy-bottomed pot on medium-high fire and heat for 2 minutes. Add oil and heat for a minute.
2. Stir in pork chunks and cook for 3 minutes per side.
3. Add ginger, cilantro, pepper, and salt. Sauté for 2 minutes.
4. Add water and deglaze the pot. Stir in 5-spice powder.
5. Cover and simmer for 20 minutes.
6. Stir in coconut milk. Cover and cook for another 10 minutes.
7. Adjust seasoning if needed.
8. Serve and enjoy.

Nutrition Info:

- Per Servings 4.4g Carbs, 39.8g Protein, 30.5g Fat, 398 Calories

New York Strip Steak With Mushroom Sauce

Servings: 2 | Cooking Time: 20 Minutes

Ingredients:

- 2 New York Strip steaks, trimmed from fat
- 3 cloves of garlic, minced
- 2 ounces shiitake mushrooms, sliced
- 2 ounces button mushrooms, sliced
- ¼ teaspoon thyme
- ¼ cup water
- ½ tsp salt
- 1 tsp pepper
- 5 tablespoons olive oil

Directions:

1. Heat the grill to 350F.
2. Position the grill rack 6 inches from the heat source.
3. Grill the steak for 10 minutes on each side or until slightly pink on the inside.
4. Meanwhile, prepare the sauce. In a small nonstick pan, water sauté the garlic, mushrooms, salt, pepper, and thyme for a minute. Pour in the broth and bring to a boil. Allow the sauce to simmer until the liquid is reduced.
5. Top the steaks with the mushroom sauce. Drizzle with olive oil.
6. Serve warm.

Nutrition Info:

- Per Servings 4.0g Carbs, 47.0g Protein, 36.0g Fat, 528 Calories

Hot Pork With Dill Pickles

Servings: 4 | Cooking Time: 20 Minutes

Ingredients:

- ¼ cup lime juice
- 4 pork chops
- 1 tbsp coconut oil, melted
- 2 garlic cloves, minced
- 1 tbsp chili powder
- 1 tsp ground cinnamon
- 2 tsp cumin
- Salt and black pepper, to taste
- ½ tsp hot pepper sauce
- 4 dill pickles, cut into spears and squeezed

Directions:

1. Using a bowl, combine the lime juice with oil, cumin, salt, hot pepper sauce, pepper, cinnamon, garlic, and chili powder. Place in the pork chops, toss to coat, and refrigerate for 4 hours.
2. Arrange the pork on a preheated grill over medium heat, cook for 7 minutes, turn, add in the dill pickles, and cook for another 7 minutes. Split among serving plates and enjoy.

Nutrition Info:

- Per Servings 2.3g Carbs, 36g Protein, 18g Fat, 315 Calories

Beef Meatballs

Servings: 5 | Cooking Time: 45 Minutes

Ingredients:

- ½ cup pork rinds, crushed
- 1 egg
- Salt and black pepper, to taste
- 1½ pounds ground beef
- 10 ounces canned onion soup
- 1 tbsp almond flour
- ¼ cup free-sugar ketchup
- 3 tsp Worcestershire sauce
- ½ tsp dry mustard
- ¼ cup water

Directions:

1. Using a bowl, combine ⅓ cup of the onion soup with the beef, pepper, pork rinds, egg, and salt. Heat a pan over medium-high heat, shape 12 meatballs from the beef mixture, place them into the pan, and brown on both sides.
2. In a bowl, combine the rest of the soup with the almond flour, dry mustard, ketchup, Worcestershire sauce, and water. Pour this over the beef meatballs, cover the pan, and cook for 20 minutes as you stir occasionally. Split among serving bowls and enjoy.

Nutrition Info:

- Per Servings 7g Carbs, 25g Protein, 18g Fat, 332 Calories

Slow Cooker Pork

Servings: 10 | Cooking Time: 10 Hours

Ingredients:

- 3 lb. boneless pork loin roast
- ¼ cup Dijon mustard
- 1 tsp. dried thyme leaves
- 2 bay leaves
- 5 tablespoons olive oil
- Salt and pepper to taste
- 1 ½ cups water

Directions:

1. Place all ingredients in the slow cooker.
2. Season with salt and pepper and give a good stir.
3. Cover and cook on low for 10 hours.
4. Serve and enjoy.

Nutrition Info:

- Per Servings 0.4g Carbs, 30.7g Protein, 15.7g Fat, 245 Calories

Italian Sausage Stew

Servings: 6 | Cooking Time: 35 Minutes

Ingredients:

- 1 pound Italian sausage, sliced
- 1 red bell pepper, seeded and chopped
- 2 onions, chopped
- Salt and black pepper, to taste
- 1 cup fresh parsley, chopped
- 6 green onions, chopped
- ¼ cup avocado oil
- 1 cup beef stock
- 4 garlic cloves
- 24 ounces canned diced tomatoes
- 16 ounces okra, trimmed and sliced
- 6 ounces tomato sauce
- 2 tbsp coconut aminos
- 1 tbsp hot sauce

Directions:

1. Set a pot over medium-high heat and warm oil, place in the sausages, and cook for 2 minutes. Stir in the onion, green onions, garlic, pepper, bell pepper, and salt, and cook for 5 minutes.
2. Add in the hot sauce, stock, tomatoes, coconut aminos, okra, and tomato sauce, bring to a simmer and cook for 15 minutes. Adjust the seasoning with salt and pepper. Share into serving bowls and sprinkle with fresh parsley to serve.

Nutrition Info:

- Per Servings 7g Carbs, 16g Protein, 25g Fat, 314 Calories

Beef Cauliflower Curry

Servings: 6 | Cooking Time: 26 Minutes

Ingredients:

- 1 tbsp olive oil
- 1 ½ lb ground beef
- 1 tbsp ginger-garlic paste
- 1 tsp garam masala
- 1 can whole tomatoes
- 1 head cauliflower, cut into florets
- Pink salt and chili pepper to taste
- ¼ cup water

Directions:

1. Heat oil in a saucepan over medium heat, add the beef, ginger-garlic paste and season with garam masala. Cook for 5 minutes while breaking any lumps.
2. Stir in the tomatoes and cauliflower, season with salt and chili pepper, and cook covered for 6 minutes. Add the water and bring to a boil over medium heat for 10 minutes or until the water has reduced by half. Adjust taste with salt.
3. Spoon the curry into serving bowls and serve with shirataki rice.

Nutrition Info:

- Per Servings 2g Carbs, 22g Protein, 33g Fat, 374 Calories

Caribbean Beef

Servings: 8 | Cooking Time: 1 Hour 10 Minutes

Ingredients:

- 2 onions, chopped
- 2 tbsp avocado oil
- 2 pounds beef stew meat, cubed
- 2 red bell peppers, seeded and chopped
- 1 habanero pepper, chopped
- 4 green chilies, chopped
- 14.5 ounces canned diced tomatoes
- 2 tbsp fresh cilantro, chopped
- 4 garlic cloves, minced
- ½ cup vegetable broth
- Salt and black pepper, to taste
- 1 ½ tsp cumin
- ½ cup black olives, chopped
- 1 tsp dried oregano

Directions:

1. Set a pan over medium-high heat and warm avocado oil. Brown the beef on all sides; remove and set aside. Stir-fry in the red bell peppers, green chilies, oregano, garlic, habanero pepper, onions, and cumin, for about 5-6 minutes. Pour in the tomatoes and broth, and cook for 1 hour. Stir in the olives, adjust the seasonings and serve in bowls sprinkled with fresh cilantro.

Nutrition Info:

- Per Servings 8g Carbs, 25g Protein, 14g Fat, 305 Calories

Old-style Beef Stew

Servings: 5 | Cooking Time: 40 Minutes

Ingredients:

- 1 ½-pounds beef stew meat, cubed into 1-inch squares
- 16-ounce fresh cremini mushrooms
- 3 medium tomatoes, chopped
- 1 envelope reduced-sodium onion soup mix
- 5 tablespoons butter
- 1 cup water
- Pepper and salt to taste

Directions:

1. Add all ingredients in a pot on high fire and bring to a boil.
2. Once boiling, lower fire to a simmer and cook for 25 minutes.
3. Adjust seasoning to taste.
4. Serve and enjoy.

Nutrition Info:

- Per Servings 11.5g Carbs, 58g Protein, 27.8g Fat, 551 Calories

Ribeye Steak With Shitake Mushrooms

Servings: 1 | Cooking Time: 25 Minutes

Ingredients:

- 6 ounces ribeye steak
- 2 tbsp butter
- 1 tsp olive oil
- ½ cup shitake mushrooms, sliced
- Salt and ground pepper, to taste

Directions:

1. Heat the olive oil in a pan over medium heat. Rub the steak with salt and pepper and cook about 4 minutes per side; set aside. Melt the butter in the pan and cook the shitakes for 4 minutes. Pour the butter and mushrooms over the steak to serve.

Nutrition Info:

- Per Servings 3g Carbs, 33g Protein, 31g Fat, 478 Calories

Italian Shredded Beef

Servings: 6 | Cooking Time: 42 Minutes

Ingredients:

- 3 pounds chuck roast, trimmed from excess fat and cut into chunks
- 1 packet Italian salad dressing mix
- 8 ounces pepperoncini pepper slices
- 1 can beef broth
- Salt and pepper to taste
- 1 cup water
- 1 tsp oil

Directions:

1. Place a heavy-bottomed pot on medium-high fire and heat for 2 minutes. Add oil and swirl to coat the bottom and sides of pot and heat for a minute.
2. Season roast with pepper and salt. Brown roast for 4 minutes per side. Transfer to a chopping board and chop into 4 equal pieces.
3. Add remaining ingredients to the pot along with sliced beef.
4. Cover and simmer for 30 minutes or until beef is fork-tender. Stir the bottom of the pot now and then. Turn off the fire.
5. With two forks, shred beef.
6. Turn on fire to high and boil uncovered until sauce is rendered, around 5 minutes.

Nutrition Info:

- Per Servings 6.6g Carbs, 61.5g Protein, 20.5g Fat, 455 Calories

Easy Zucchini Beef Lasagna

Servings: 4 | Cooking Time: 1 Hour 15 Minutes

Ingredients:

- 1 lb ground beef
- 2 large zucchinis, sliced lengthwise
- 3 cloves garlic
- 1 medium white onion, finely chopped
- 3 tomatoes, chopped
- Salt and black pepper to taste
- 2 tsp sweet paprika
- 1 tsp dried thyme
- 1 tsp dried basil
- 1 cup shredded mozzarella cheese
- 1 tbsp olive oil
- Cooking spray

Directions:

1. Preheat the oven to 370ºF and lightly grease a baking dish with cooking spray.
2. Lay the zucchini slices on a paper towel and sprinkle with salt. Set aside.
3. Heat the olive oil in a skillet and cook the beef for 4 minutes while breaking any lumps as you stir. Top with onion, garlic, tomatoes, salt, paprika, and pepper. Stir and continue cooking for 5 minutes.
4. Then, back to the zucchinis, use a paper towel to blot out any liquid on it and lay ⅓ of the slices in the baking dish. Top with ⅓ of the beef mixture and repeat the layering process two more times with the same quantities. Season with basil and thyme.
5. Finally, sprinkle the mozzarella cheese on top and tuck the baking dish in the oven. Bake for 35 minutes. Remove the lasagna and let it rest for 10 minutes before serving.

Nutrition Info:

- Per Servings 2.9g Carbs, 40.4g Protein, 17.8g Fat, 344 Calories

Simple Beef Curry

Servings: 6 | Cooking Time:30 Minutes

Ingredients:

- 2 pounds boneless beef chuck
- 1 tbsp ground turmeric
- 1 tsp ginger paste
- 6 cloves garlic, minced
- 1 onion, chopped
- 3 tbsp olive oil
- 1 cup water
- Pepper and salt to taste

Directions:

1. In a saucepan, heat the olive oil over medium heat then add onion and garlic for 5 minutes.
2. Stir in beef and sauté for 10 minutes.
3. Add remaining ingredients, cover, and simmer for 20 minutes.
4. Adjust seasoning if needed.
5. Serve and enjoy.

Nutrition Info:

- Per Servings 5.0g Carbs, 33.0g Protein, 16.0g Fat, 287 Calories

Peanut Butter Pork Stir-fry

Servings: 4 | Cooking Time: 23 Minutes

Ingredients:

- 1 ½ tbsp ghee
- 2 lb pork loin, cut into strips
- Pink salt and chili pepper to taste
- 2 tsp ginger- garlic paste
- ¼ cup chicken broth
- 5 tbsp peanut butter
- 2 cups mixed stir-fry vegetables

Directions:

1. Melt the ghee in a wok and mix the pork with salt, chili pepper, and ginger-garlic paste. Pour the pork into the wok and cook for 6 minutes until no longer pink.
2. Mix the peanut butter with some broth to be smooth, add to the pork and stir; cook for 2 minutes. Pour in the remaining broth, cook for 4 minutes, and add the mixed veggies. Simmer for 5 minutes.
3. Adjust the taste with salt and black pepper, and spoon the stir-fry to a side of cilantro cauli rice.

Nutrition Info:

- Per Servings 1g Carbs, 22.5g Protein, 49g Fat, 571 Calories

Beef And Butternut Squash Stew

Servings: 4 | Cooking Time: 40 Minutes

Ingredients:

- 3 tsp olive oil
- 1 pound ground beef
- 1 cup beef stock
- 14 ounces canned tomatoes with juice
- 1 tbsp stevia
- 1 pound butternut squash, chopped
- 1 tbsp Worcestershire sauce
- 2 bay leaves
- Salt and ground black pepper, to taste
- 3 tbsp fresh parsley, chopped
- 1 onion, chopped
- 1 tsp dried sage
- 1 tbsp garlic, minced

Directions:

1. Set a pan over medium heat and heat olive oil, stir in the onion, garlic, and beef, and cook for 10 minutes. Add in butternut squash, Worcestershire sauce, bay leaves, stevia, beef stock, canned tomatoes, and sage, and bring to a boil. Reduce heat, and simmer for 20 minutes.
2. Adjust the seasonings. Split into bowls and enjoy.

Nutrition Info:

- Per Servings 7.3g Carbs, 32g Protein, 17g Fat, 343 Calories

Pork Goulash With Cauliflower

Servings: 4 | Cooking Time: 15 Minutes

Ingredients:

- 1 red bell pepper, seeded and chopped
- 2 tbsp olive oil
- 1½ pounds ground pork
- Salt and black pepper, to taste
- 2 cups cauliflower florets
- 1 onion, chopped
- 14 ounces canned diced tomatoes
- ¼ tsp garlic powder
- 1 tbsp tomato puree
- 1 ½ cups water

Directions:

1. Heat olive oil in a pan over medium heat, stir in the pork, and brown for 5 minutes. Place in the bell pepper and onion, and cook for 4 minutes. Stir in the water, tomatoes, and cauliflower, bring to a simmer and cook for 5 minutes while covered. Place in the pepper, tomato paste, salt, and garlic powder. Stir well, remove from the heat, split into bowls, and enjoy with keto bread.

Nutrition Info:

- Per Servings 4.5g Carbs, 44g Protein, 37g Fat, 475 Calories

Beef And Egg Rice Bowls

Servings: 4 | Cooking Time: 22 Minutes

Ingredients:

- 2 cups cauli rice
- 3 cups frozen mixed vegetables
- 3 tbsp ghee
- 1 lb skirt steak
- Salt and black pepper to taste
- 4 fresh eggs
- Hot sauce (sugar-free) for topping

Directions:

1. Mix the cauli rice and mixed vegetables in a bowl, sprinkle with a little water, and steam in the microwave for 1 minute to be tender. Share into 4 serving bowls.
2. Melt the ghee in a skillet, season the beef with salt and pepper, and brown for 5 minutes on each side. Use a perforated spoon to ladle the meat onto the vegetables.
3. Wipe out the skillet and return to medium heat, crack in an egg, season with salt and pepper and cook until the egg white has set, but the yolk is still runny 3 minutes. Remove egg onto the vegetable bowl and fry the remaining 3 eggs. Add to the other bowls.
4. Drizzle the beef bowls with hot sauce and serve.

Nutrition Info:

- Per Servings 4g Carbs, 15g Protein, 26g Fat, 320 Calories

Pork Nachos

Servings: 4 | Cooking Time: 15 Minutes

Ingredients:
- 1 bag low carb tortilla chips
- 2 cups leftover pulled pork
- 1 red bell pepper, seeded and chopped
- 1 red onion, diced
- 2 cups shredded Monterey Jack cheese

Directions:

1. Preheat oven to 350ºF. Arrange the chips in a medium cast iron pan, scatter pork over, followed by red bell pepper, and onion, and sprinkle with cheese. Place the pan in the oven and cook for 10 minutes until the cheese has melted. Allow cooling for 3 minutes and serve.

Nutrition Info:
- Per Servings 9.3g Carbs, 22g Protein, 25g Fat, 452 Calories

Beef Sausage Casserole

Servings: 8 | Cooking Time: 60 Minutes

Ingredients:
- ⅓ cup almond flour
- 2 eggs
- 2 pounds beef sausage, chopped
- Salt and black pepper, to taste
- 1 tbsp dried parsley
- ¼ tsp red pepper flakes
- ¼ cup Parmesan cheese, grated
- ¼ tsp onion powder
- ½ tsp garlic powder
- ¼ tsp dried oregano
- 1 cup ricotta cheese
- 1 cup sugar-free marinara sauce
- 1½ cups cheddar cheese, shredded

Directions:

1. Using a bowl, combine the sausage, pepper, pepper flakes, oregano, eggs, Parmesan cheese, onion powder, almond flour, salt, parsley, and garlic powder. Form balls, lay them on a lined baking sheet, place in the oven at 370ºF, and bake for 15 minutes.

2. Remove the balls from the oven and cover with half of the marinara sauce. Pour ricotta cheese all over followed by the rest of the marinara sauce. Scatter the cheddar cheese and bake in the oven for 10 minutes. Allow the meatballs casserole to cool before serving.

Nutrition Info:
- Per Servings 4g Carbs, 32g Protein, 35g Fat, 456 Calories

Beef And Feta Salad

Servings: 4 | Cooking Time: 35 Minutes

Ingredients:

- 3 tbsp olive oil
- ½ pound beef rump steak, cut into strips
- Salt and ground black pepper, to taste
- 1 tsp cumin
- A pinch of dried thyme
- 2 garlic cloves, minced
- 4 ounces feta cheese, crumbled
- ½ cup pecans, toasted
- 2 cups spinach
- 1½ tbsp lemon juice
- ¼ cup fresh mint, chopped

Directions:

1. Season the beef with salt, 1 tbsp of olive oil, garlic, thyme, black pepper, and cumin. Place on preheated grill over medium-high heat, and cook for 10 minutes, flip once. Sprinkle the pecans on a lined baking sheet, place in the oven at 350ºF, and toast for 10 minutes.
2. Remove the grilled beef to a cutting board, leave to cool, and slice into strips.
3. In a salad bowl, combine the spinach with pepper, mint, remaining olive oil, salt, lemon juice, feta cheese, and pecans, and toss well to coat. Top with the beef slices and enjoy.

Nutrition Info:

- Per Servings 3.5g Carbs, 17g Protein, 43g Fat, 434 Calories

Spiced Pork Roast With Collard Greens

Servings: 4 | Cooking Time: 40 Minutes

Ingredients:

- 2 tbsp olive oil
- Salt and black pepper, to taste
- 1 ½ pounds pork loin
- A pinch of dry mustard
- 1 tsp hot red pepper flakes
- ½ tsp ginger, minced
- 1 cup collard greens, chopped
- 2 garlic cloves, minced
- ½ lemon sliced
- ¼ cup water

Directions:

1. Using a bowl, combine the ginger with salt, mustard, and pepper. Add in the meat, toss to coat. Heat the oil in a saucepan over medium-high heat, brown the pork on all sides, for 10 minutes.
2. Transfer to the oven and roast for 1 hour at 390 F. To the saucepan, add collard greens, lemon slices, garlic, and water; cook for 10 minutes. Serve on a platter, sprinkle pan juices on top and enjoy.

Nutrition Info:

- Per Servings 3g Carbs, 45g Protein, 23g Fat, 430 Calories

Beef Steak Filipino Style

Servings: 6 | Cooking Time: 25 Minutes

Ingredients:

- 2 tablespoons coconut oil
- 1 onion, sliced
- 4 beef steaks
- 2 tablespoons lemon juice, freshly squeezed
- ¼ cup coconut aminos
- 1 tsp salt
- Pepper to taste

Directions:

1. In a nonstick fry pan, heat oil on medium-high fire.
2. Pan-fry beef steaks and season with coconut aminos.
3. Cook until dark brown, around 7 minutes per side. Transfer to a plate.
4. Sauté onions in the same pan until caramelized, around 8 minutes. Season with lemon juice and return steaks in the pan. Mix well.
5. Serve and enjoy.

Nutrition Info:

- Per Servings 0.7g Carbs, 25.3g Protein, 27.1g Fat, 347 Calories

Dr. Pepper Pulled Pork

Servings: 9 | Cooking Time: 45 Minutes

Ingredients:

- 3 pounds pork loin roast, chopped into 8 equal pieces
- 1 packet pork rub seasoning
- 1 12-ounce can Dr. Pepper
- ½ cup commercial BBQ sauce
- 1 bay leaf
- 1 tsp oil
- 2 tbsp water

Directions:

1. Place a heavy-bottomed pot on medium-high fire and heat for 2 minutes. Add oil and swirl to coat the bottom and sides of pot and heat for a minute.
2. Brown roast for 4 minutes per side.
3. Add remaining ingredients.
4. Cover and simmer for 30 minutes or until pork is fork-tender. Stir the bottom of the pot every now and then. Turn off the fire.
5. With two forks, shred pork.
6. Turn on fire to high and boil uncovered until sauce is rendered, around 5 minutes.
7. Serve and enjoy.

Nutrition Info:

- Per Servings 4.6g Carbs, 40.9g Protein, 13.4g Fat, 310 Calories

Beef Zucchini Boats

Servings: 4 | Cooking Time: 45 Minutes

Ingredients:

- 2 garlic cloves, minced
- 1 tsp cumin
- 1 tbsp olive oil
- 1 pound ground beef
- ½ cup onion, chopped
- 1 tsp smoked paprika
- Salt and ground black pepper, to taste
- 4 zucchinis
- ¼ cup fresh cilantro, chopped
- ½ cup Monterey Jack cheese, shredded
- 1½ cups enchilada sauce
- 1 avocado, chopped, for serving
- Green onions, chopped, for serving
- Tomatoes, chopped, for serving

Directions:

1. Set a pan over high heat and warm the oil. Add the onions, and cook for 2 minutes. Stir in the beef, and brown for 4-5 minutes. Stir in the paprika, pepper, garlic, cumin, and salt; cook for 2 minutes.

2. Slice the zucchini in half lengthwise and scoop out the seeds. Set the zucchini in a greased baking pan, stuff each with the beef, scatter enchilada sauce on top, and spread with the Monterey cheese.

3. Bake in the oven at 350ºF for 20 minutes while covered. Uncover, spread with cilantro, and bake for 5 minutes. Top with tomatoes, green onions and avocado, place on serving plates and enjoy.

Nutrition Info:

- Per Servings 7.8g Carbs, 39g Protein, 33g Fat, 422 Calories

Chapter 6 Fish And Seafood Recipes

Chapter 6 Fish And Seafood Recipes

Sautéed Savory Shrimps

Servings: 8 | Cooking Time: 15 Minutes

Ingredients:

- 2 pounds shrimp, peeled and deveined
- 4 cloves garlic, minced
- ½ cup chicken stock, low sodium
- 1 tablespoon lemon juice
- Salt and pepper
- 5 tablespoons oil

Directions:

1. Place a heavy-bottomed pot on medium-high fire and heat pot for 3 minutes.
2. Once hot, add oil and stir around to coat pot with oil.
3. Sauté the garlic and corn for 5 minutes.
4. Add remaining ingredients and mix well.
5. Cover and bring to a boil, lower fire to a simmer, and simmer for 5 minutes.
6. Serve and enjoy.

Nutrition Info:

- Per Servings 1.7g Carbs, 25.2g Protein, 9.8g Fat, 182.6 Calories

Alaskan Cod With Mustard Cream Sauce

Serves: 4 | Cooking Time: 10 Minutes

Ingredients:

- 1 tablespoon coconut oil
- 4 Alaskan cod fillets
- Salt and freshly ground black pepper, to taste
- 6 leaves basil, chiffonade
- Mustard Cream Sauce:
- 1 teaspoon yellow mustard
- 1 teaspoon paprika
- 1/4 teaspoon ground bay leaf
- 3 tablespoons cream cheese
- 1/2 cup Greek-style yogurt
- 1 garlic clove, minced
- 1 teaspoon lemon zest
- 1 tablespoon fresh parsley, minced
- Sea salt and ground black pepper, to taste

Directions:

1. Heat coconut oil in a pan over medium heat. Sear the fish for 2 to 3 minutes per side. Season with salt and ground black pepper.
2. Mix all ingredients for the sauce until everything is well combined. Top the fish fillets with the sauce and serve garnished with fresh basil leaves. Bon appétit!

Nutrition Info:

- Per Serves 2.6g Carbs; 19.8g Protein; 8.2g Fat; 166 Calories;

Halibut En Papillote

Servings: 4 | Cooking Time: 15 Minutes

Ingredients:

- 4 halibut fillets
- ½ tbsp. grated ginger
- 1 cup chopped tomatoes
- 1 shallot, thinly sliced
- 1 lemon
- 5 tbsp olive oil
- Salt and pepper to taste

Directions:

1. Slice lemon in half. Slice one lemon in circles.
2. Juice the other half of the lemon in a small bowl. Mix in grated ginger and season with pepper and salt.
3. Place a trivet in a large saucepan and pour a cup or two of water into the pan. Bring to a boil.
4. Get 4 large foil and place one fillet in the middle of each foil. Season with fillet salt and pepper. Drizzle with olive oil. Add the grated ginger, tomatoes, and shallots equally. Fold the foil to create a pouch and crimp the edges.
5. Place the foil containing the fish on the trivet. Cover saucepan and steam for 15 minutes.
6. Serve and enjoy in pouches.

Nutrition Info:

- Per Servings 2.7g Carbs, 20.3g Protein, 32.3g Fat, 410 Calories

Golden Pompano In Microwave

Servings: 2 | Cooking Time: 11 Minutes

Ingredients:

- ½-lb pompano
- 1 tbsp soy sauce, low sodium
- 1-inch thumb ginger, diced
- 1 lemon, halved
- 1 stalk green onions, chopped
- ¼ cup water
- 1 tsp pepper
- 4 tbsp olive oil

Directions:

1. In a microwavable casserole dish, mix well all ingredients except for pompano, green onions, and lemon.
2. Squeeze half of the lemon in dish and slice into thin circles the other half.
3. Place pompano in the dish and add lemon circles on top of the fish. Drizzle with pepper and olive oil.
4. Cover top of a casserole dish with a microwave-safe plate.
5. Microwave for 5 minutes.
6. Remove from microwave, turn over fish, sprinkle green onions, top with a microwavable plate.
7. Return to microwave and cook for another 3 minutes.
8. Let it rest for 3 minutes more.
9. Serve and enjoy.

Nutrition Info:

- Per Servings 6.3g Carbs, 22.2g Protein, 39.5g Fat, 464 Calories

Salmon With Pepita And Lime

Servings: 4 | Cooking Time: 15 Minutes

Ingredients:

- 2 tbsp. Pepitas, ground
- ¼ tsp. chili powder
- 1 lb. salmon fillet, cut into 4 portions
- 2 tbsp. lime juice
- Salt and pepper to taste

Directions:

1. Place a trivet in a large saucepan and pour a cup of water into the pan. Bring it to a boil.
2. Place salmon in a heatproof dish that fits inside a saucepan. Drizzle lime juice on the fillet. Season with salt, pepper, and chili powder. Garnish with ground pepitas.
3. Seal dish with foil. Place the dish on the trivet inside the saucepan. Cover and steam for 15 minutes.
4. Serve and enjoy.

Nutrition Info:

- Per Servings 1g Carbs, 24g Protein, 9g Fat, 185 Calories

Avocado Tuna Boats

Serves: 2 | Cooking Time: 10 Minutes

Ingredients:

- 4 oz tuna, packed in water, drained1 green onion sliced
- 1 avocado, halved, pitted
- 3 tbsp mayonnaise
- 1/3 tsp salt
- Seasoning:
- ¼ tsp ground black pepper
- ¼ tsp paprika

Directions:

1. Prepare the filling and for this, take a medium bowl, place tuna in it, add green onion, salt, black pepper, paprika and mayonnaise and then stir until well combined.Cut avocado in half lengthwise, then remove the pit and fill with prepared filling.Serve.

Nutrition Info:

- ; 7 g Carbs; 8 g Protein; 19 g Fats; 244 Calories

Enchilada Sauce On Mahi Mahi

Servings: 2 | Cooking Time: 15 Minutes

Ingredients:

- 2 Mahi fillets, fresh
- ¼ cup commercial enchilada sauce
- Pepper to taste

Directions:

1. In a heat-proof dish that fits inside saucepan, place fish and top with enchilada sauce.
2. Place a large saucepan on the medium-high fire. Place a trivet inside the saucepan and fill the pan halfway with water. Cover and bring to a boil.
3. Cover dish with foil and place on a trivet.
4. Cover pan and steam for 10 minutes. Let it rest in pan for another 5 minutes.
5. Serve and enjoy topped with pepper.

Nutrition Info:

- Per Servings 8.9g Carbs, 19.8g Protein, 15.9g Fat, 257 Calories

Coconut Crab Patties

Servings: 8 | Cooking Time: 15 Minutes

Ingredients:

- 2 tbsp coconut oil
- 1 tbsp lemon juice
- 1 cup lump crab meat
- 2 tsp Dijon mustard
- 1 egg, beaten
- 1 ½ tbsp coconut flour

Directions:

1. In a bowl to the crabmeat add all the ingredients, except for the oil; mix well to combine. Make patties out of the mixture. Melt the coconut oil in a skillet over medium heat. Add the crab patties and cook for about 2-3 minutes per side.

Nutrition Info:

- Per Servings 3.6g Carbs, 15.3g Protein, 11.5g Fat, 215 Calories

Coconut Curry Mussels

Servings: 6 | Cooking Time: 25 Minutes

Ingredients:

- 3 lb mussels, cleaned, de-bearded
- 1 cup minced shallots
- 3 tbsp minced garlic
- 1 ½ cups coconut milk
- 2 cups dry white wine
- 2 tsp red curry powder
- ⅓ cup coconut oil
- ⅓ cup chopped green onions
- ⅓ cup chopped parsley

Directions:

1. Pour the wine into a large saucepan and cook the shallots and garlic over low heat. Stir in the coconut milk and red curry powder and cook for 3 minutes.
2. Add the mussels and steam for 7 minutes or until their shells are opened. Then, use a slotted spoon to remove to a bowl leaving the sauce in the pan. Discard any closed mussels at this point.
3. Stir the coconut oil into the sauce, turn the heat off, and stir in the parsley and green onions. Serve the sauce immediately with a butternut squash mash.

Nutrition Info:

- Per Servings 0.3g Carbs, 21.1g Protein, 20.6g Fat, 356 Calories

Lemon Chili Halibut

Servings: 2 | Cooking Time: 15 Minutes

Ingredients:

- 1-lb halibut fillets
- 1 lemon, sliced
- 1 tablespoon chili pepper flakes
- Pepper and salt to taste
- 4 tbsp olive oil

Directions:

1. In a heat-proof dish that fits inside saucepan, place fish. Top fish with chili flakes, lemon slices, salt, and pepper. Drizzle with olive oil. Cover dish with foil
2. Place a large saucepan on the medium-high fire. Place a trivet inside the saucepan and fill the pan halfway with water. Cover and bring to a boil.
3. Place dish on the trivet.
4. Cover pan and steam for 10 minutes. Let it rest in pan for another 5 minutes.
5. Serve and enjoy topped with pepper.

Nutrition Info:

- Per Servings 4.2g Carbs, 42.7g Protein, 58.4g Fat, 675 Calories

Halibut With Pesto

Servings: 4 | Cooking Time: 15 Minutes

Ingredients:

- 4 halibut fillets
- 1 cup basil leaves
- 2 cloves of garlic, minced
- 1 tbsp. lemon juice, freshly squeezed
- 2 tbsp pine nuts
- 2 tbsp. oil, preferably extra virgin olive oil
- Salt and pepper to taste

Directions:

1. In a food processor, pulse the basil, olive oil, pine nuts, garlic, and lemon juice until coarse. Season with salt and pepper to taste.
2. Place a trivet in a large saucepan and pour a cup or two of water into the pan. Bring to a boil.
3. Place salmon in a heatproof dish that fits inside a saucepan. Season salmon with pepper and salt. Drizzle with pesto sauce.
4. Seal dish with foil. Place the dish on the trivet inside the saucepan. Cover and steam for 15 minutes.
5. Serve and enjoy.

Nutrition Info:

- Per Servings 0.8g Carbs, 75.8g Protein, 8.4g Fat, 401 Calories

Coconut Milk Sauce Over Crabs

Servings: 6 | Cooking Time: 20 Minutes

Ingredients:

- 2-pounds crab quartered
- 1 can coconut milk
- 1 thumb-size ginger, sliced
- 1 onion, chopped
- 3 cloves of garlic, minced
- Pepper and salt to taste

Directions:

1. Place a heavy-bottomed pot on medium-high fire and add all ingredients.
2. Cover and bring to a boil, lower fire to a simmer, and simmer for 20 minutes.
3. Serve and enjoy.

Nutrition Info:

- Per Servings 6.3g Carbs, 29.3g Protein, 11.3g Fat, 244.1 Calories

Steamed Herbed Red Snapper

Servings: 4 | Cooking Time: 15 Minutes

Ingredients:

- 4 red snapper fillets
- ¼ tsp. paprika
- 3 tbsp. lemon juice, freshly squeezed
- 1 ½ tsp chopped fresh herbs of your choice (rosemary, thyme, basil, or parsley)
- 6 tbsp olive oil
- Salt and pepper to taste

Directions:

1. In a small bowl, whisk well paprika, lemon juice, olive oil, and herbs. Season with pepper and salt.
2. Place a trivet in a large saucepan and pour a cup or two of water into the pan. Bring to a boil.
3. Place snapper in a heatproof dish that fits inside a saucepan. Season snapper with pepper and salt. Drizzle with lemon mixture.
4. Seal dish with foil. Place the dish on the trivet inside the saucepan. Cover and steam for 15 minutes.
5. Serve and enjoy.

Nutrition Info:

- Per Servings 2.1g Carbs, 45.6g Protein, 20.3g Fat, 374 Calories

Cod With Balsamic Tomatoes

Servings: 4 | Cooking Time: 30 Minutes

Ingredients:

- 4 center-cut bacon strips, chopped
- 4 cod fillets
- 2 cups grape tomatoes, halved
- 2 tablespoons balsamic vinegar
- 4 tablespoons olive oil
- 1/2 teaspoon salt
- 1/4 teaspoon pepper

Directions:

1. In a large skillet, heat olive oil and cook bacon over medium heat until crisp, stirring occasionally.
2. Remove with a slotted spoon; drain on paper towels.
3. Sprinkle fillets with salt and pepper. Add fillets to bacon drippings; cook over medium-high heat until fish just begins to flake easily with a fork, 4-6 minutes on each side. Remove and keep warm.
4. Add tomatoes to skillet; cook and stir until tomatoes are softened, 2-4 minutes. Stir in vinegar; reduce heat to medium-low. Cook until sauce is thickened, 1-2 minutes longer.
5. Serve cod with tomato mixture and bacon.

Nutrition Info:

- Per Servings 5g Carbs, 26g Protein, 30.4g Fat, 442 Calories

Steamed Asparagus And Shrimps

Servings: 6 | Cooking Time: 15 Minutes

Ingredients:

- 1-pound shrimps, peeled and deveined
- 1 bunch asparagus, trimmed
- ½ tablespoon Cajun seasoning
- 2 tablespoons butter
- 5 tablespoons oil
- Salt and pepper to taste

Directions:

1. In a heat-proof dish that fits inside the saucepan, add all ingredients. Mix well.
2. Place a large saucepan on the medium-high fire. Place a trivet inside the saucepan and fill the pan halfway with water. Cover and bring to a boil.
3. Cover dish with foil and place on a trivet.
4. Cover pan and steam for 10 minutes. Let it rest in pan for another 5 minutes.
5. Serve and enjoy.

Nutrition Info:

- Per Servings 1.1g Carbs, 15.5g Protein, 15.8g Fat, 204.8 Calories

Creamy Hoki With Almond Bread Crust

Servings: 4 | Cooking Time: 50 Minutes

Ingredients:

- 1 cup flaked smoked hoki, bones removed
- 1 cup cubed hoki fillets, cubed
- 4 eggs
- 1 cup water
- 3 tbsp almond flour
- 1 medium white onion, sliced
- 2 cups sour cream
- 1 tbsp chopped parsley
- 1 cup pork rinds, crushed
- 1 cup grated cheddar cheese
- Salt and black pepper to taste
- Cooking spray

Directions:

1. Preheat the oven to 360ºF and lightly grease a baking dish with cooking spray.
2. Then, boil the eggs in water in a pot over medium heat to be well done for 12 minutes, run the eggs under cold water and peel the shells. After, place on a cutting board and chop them.
3. Melt the butter in a saucepan over medium heat and sauté the onion for about 4 minutes. Turn the heat off and stir the almond flour into it to form a roux. Turn the heat back on and cook the roux to be golden brown and stir in the cream until the mixture is smooth. Season with salt and pepper, and stir in the parsley.
4. Spread the smoked and cubed fish in the baking dish, sprinkle the eggs on top, and spoon the sauce over. In a bowl, mix the pork rinds with the cheddar cheese, and sprinkle it over the sauce.
5. Bake the casserole in the oven for 20 minutes until the top is golden and the sauce and cheese are bubbly. Remove the bake after and serve with a steamed green vegetable mix.

Nutrition Info:

- Per Servings 3.5g Carbs, 28.5g Protein, 27g Fat, 386 Calories

Baked Cod And Tomato Capers Mix

Serves: 4 | Cooking Time: 25 Minutes

Ingredients:

- 4 cod fillets, boneless
- 2 tablespoons avocado oil
- 1 cup tomato passata
- 2 tablespoons capers, drained
- 2 tablespoons parsley, choppedA pinch of salt and black pepper

Directions:

1. In a roasting pan, combine the cod with the oil and the other ingredients, toss gently, introduce in the oven at 370 °F and bake for 25 minutes.
2. Divide between plates and serve.

Nutrition Info:

- 0.7g carbs; 2g fat; 5g protein; 150 calories

Simple Steamed Salmon Fillets

Servings: 3 | Cooking Time: 15 Minutes

Ingredients:

- 10 oz. salmon fillets
- 2 tbsp. coconut aminos
- 2 tbsp. lemon juice, freshly squeezed
- 1 tsp. sesame seeds, toasted
- 3 tbsp sesame oil
- Salt and pepper to taste

Directions:

1. Place a trivet in a large saucepan and pour a cup or two of water into the pan. Bring to a boil.
2. Place salmon in a heatproof dish that fits inside the saucepan. Season salmon with pepper and salt. Drizzle with coconut aminos, lemon juice, sesame oil, and sesame seeds.
3. Seal dish with foil. Place the dish on the trivet inside the saucepan. Cover and steam for 15 minutes.
4. Serve and enjoy.

Nutrition Info:

- Per Servings 2.6g Carbs, 20.1g Protein, 17.4g Fat, 210 Calories

Baked Fish With Feta And Tomato

Serves: 2 | Cooking Time: 15 Minutes

Ingredients:

- 2 pacific whitening fillets
- 1 scallion, chopped
- 1 Roma tomato, chopped
- 1 tsp fresh oregano
- 1-ounce feta cheese, crumbled
- Seasoning:
- 2 tbsp avocado oil
- 1/3 tsp salt
- 1/4 tsp ground black pepper
- ¼ crushed red pepper

Directions:

1. Turn on the oven, then set it to 400 °F and let it preheat. Take a medium skillet pan, place it over medium heat, add oil and when hot, add scallion and cook for 3 minutes. Add tomatoes, stir in ½ tsp oregano, 1/8 tsp salt, black pepper, red pepper, pour in ¼ cup water and bring it to simmer. Sprinkle remaining salt over fillets, add to the pan, drizzle with remaining oil, and then bake for 10 to 12 minutes until fillets are fork-tender. When done, top fish with remaining oregano and cheese and then serve.

Nutrition Info:

- 8 g Carbs; 26.7 g Protein; 29.5 g Fats; 427.5 Calories

Chili-garlic Salmon

Servings: 4 | Cooking Time: 15 Minutes

Ingredients:

- 5 tbsp. sweet chili sauce
- ¼ cup coconut aminos
- 4 salmon fillets
- 3 tbsp. green onions, chopped
- 3 cloves garlic, peeled and minced
- Pepper to taste

Directions:

1. Place a trivet in a large saucepan and pour a cup or two of water into the pan. Bring to a boil.
2. In a small bowl, whisk well sweet chili sauce, garlic, and coconut aminos.
3. Place salmon in a heatproof dish that fits inside a saucepan. Season salmon with pepper. Drizzle with sweet chili sauce mixture. Sprinkle green onions on top of the filet.
4. Seal dish with foil. Place the dish on the trivet inside the saucepan. Cover and steam for 15 minutes.
5. Serve and enjoy.

Nutrition Info:

- Per Servings 0.9g Carbs, 65.4g Protein, 14.4g Fat, 409 Calories

Blackened Fish Tacos With Slaw

Servings: 4 | Cooking Time: 20 Minutes

Ingredients:

- 1 tbsp olive oil
- 1 tsp chili powder
- 2 tilapia fillets
- 1 tsp paprika
- 4 low carb tortillas
- Slaw:
- ½ cup red cabbage, shredded
- 1 tbsp lemon juice
- 1 tsp apple cider vinegar
- 1 tbsp olive oil

Directions:

1. Season the tilapia with chili powder and paprika. Heat the olive oil in a skillet over medium heat.
2. Add tilapia and cook until blackened, about 3 minutes per side. Cut into strips. Divide the tilapia between the tortillas. Combine all slaw ingredients in a bowl. Split the slaw among the tortillas.

Nutrition Info:

- Per Servings 3.5g Carbs, 13.8g Protein, 20g Fat, 268 Calories

Lemon-rosemary Shrimps

Servings: 4 | Cooking Time: 12 Minutes

Ingredients:

- ½ cup lemon juice, freshly squeezed
- 1 ½ lb. shrimps, peeled and deveined
- 2 tbsp fresh rosemary
- ¼ cup coconut aminos
- 2 tbsp butter
- Pepper to taste
- 4 tbsp olive oil

Directions:

1. Place a nonstick saucepan on medium-high fire and heat oil and butter for 2 minutes.
2. Stir in shrimps and coconut aminos. Season with pepper. Sauté for 5 minutes.
3. Add remaining ingredients and cook for another 5 minutes while stirring frequently.
4. Serve and enjoy.

Nutrition Info:

- Per Servings 3.7g Carbs, 35.8g Protein, 22.4g Fat, 359 Calories

Parmesan Fish Bake

Servings: 4 | Cooking Time: 40 Minutes

Ingredients:

- Cooking spray
- 2 salmon fillets, cubed
- 3 white fish, cubed
- 1 broccoli, cut into florets
- 1 tbsp butter, melted
- Pink salt and black pepper to taste
- 1 cup crème fraiche
- ¼ cup grated Parmesan cheese
- Grated Parmesan cheese for topping

Directions:

1. Preheat oven to 400ºF and grease an 8 x 8 inches casserole dish with cooking spray. Toss the fish cubes and broccoli in butter and season with salt and pepper to taste. Spread in the greased dish.
2. Mix the crème fraiche with Parmesan cheese, pour and smear the cream on the fish, and sprinkle with some more Parmesan. Bake for 25 to 30 minutes until golden brown on top, take the dish out, sit for 5 minutes and spoon into plates. Serve with lemon-mustard asparagus.

Nutrition Info:

- Per Servings 4g Carbs, 28g Protein, 17g Fat, 354 Calories

Steamed Chili-rubbed Tilapia

Servings: 4 | Cooking Time: 15 Minutes

Ingredients:

- 1 lb. tilapia fillet, skin removed
- 2 tbsp. chili powder
- 3 cloves garlic, peeled and minced
- 2 tbsp. extra virgin olive oil
- 2 tbsp soy sauce

Directions:

1. Place a trivet in a large saucepan and pour a cup or two of water into the pan. Bring it to a boil.
2. Place tilapia in a heatproof dish that fits inside a saucepan. Drizzle soy sauce and oil on the filet. Season with chili powder and garlic.
3. Seal dish with foil. Place the dish on the trivet inside the saucepan. Cover and steam for 15 minutes.
4. Serve and enjoy.

Nutrition Info:

- Per Servings 2g Carbs, 26g Protein, 10g Fat, 211 Calories

Steamed Mustard Salmon

Servings: 4 | Cooking Time: 15 Minutes

Ingredients:

- 2 tbsp Dijon mustard
- 1 whole lemon
- 2 cloves of garlic, minced
- 4 salmon fillets, skin removed
- 1 tbsp dill weed
- Salt and pepper to taste

Directions:

1. Slice lemon in half. Slice one lemon in circles and juice the other half in a small bowl.
2. Whisk in mustard, garlic, and dill weed in a bowl of lemon. Season with pepper and salt.
3. Place a trivet in a large saucepan and pour a cup or two of water into the pan. Bring to a boil.
4. Place lemon slices in a heatproof dish that fits inside a saucepan. Season salmon with pepper and salt. Slather mustard mixture on top of salmon.
5. Seal dish with foil. Place the dish on the trivet inside the saucepan. Cover and steam for 15 minutes.
6. Serve and enjoy.

Nutrition Info:

- Per Servings 2.2g Carbs, 65.3g Protein, 14.8g Fat, 402 Calories

Chapter 7 Soups, Stew & Salads Recipes

Chapter 7 Soups, Stew & Salads Recipes

Easy Tomato Salad

Servings: 4 | Cooking Time: 0 Minutes

Ingredients:

- 1 ½ cups cherry tomatoes, sliced
- ¼ cup white wine vinegar
- 1/8 cup chives
- 3 tablespoons olive oil
- Salt and pepper to taste

Directions:

1. Put all ingredients in a bowl.
2. Toss to combine.
3. Serve immediately.

Nutrition Info:

- Per Servings 0.6g Carbs, 0.3g Protein, 10.1g Fat, 95 Calories

Butternut And Kale Soup

Servings: 10 | Cooking Time: 30 Minutes

Ingredients:

- 1 package Italian turkey sausage links, casings removed
- ½ medium butternut squash, peeled and cubed
- 2 cartons reduced-sodium chicken broth
- 1 bunch kale, trimmed and coarsely chopped
- 1/2 cup shaved Parmesan cheese
- 6 tablespoons butter
- Water
- Salt to taste

Directions:

1. In a stockpot, cook sausage over medium heat until no longer pink, breaking into crumbles, 8-10 minutes.
2. Add squash and broth; bring to a boil. Gradually stir in kale, allowing it to wilt slightly between additions. Return to a boil.
3. Reduce heat; simmer, uncovered, until vegetables are tender, 15-20 minutes. Top servings with cheese.

Nutrition Info:

- Per Servings 5.3g Carbs, 13g Protein, 5g Fat, 118 Calories

Watermelon And Cucumber Salad

Servings: 10 | Cooking Time: 0 Minutes

Ingredients:

- ½ large watermelon, diced
- 1 cucumber, peeled and diced
- 1 red onion, chopped
- ¼ cup feta cheese
- ½ cup heavy cream
- Salt to taste
- 5 tbsp MCT or coconut oil

Directions:

1. Place all ingredients in a bowl.
2. Toss everything to coat.
3. Place in the fridge to cool before serving.

Nutrition Info:

- Per Servings 2.5g Carbs, 0.9g Protein, 100g Fat, 910 Calories

Bacon Chowder

Servings: 6 | Cooking Time: 15 Minutes

Ingredients:

- 1-pound bacon strips, chopped
- 1/4 cup chopped onion
- 1 can evaporated milk
- 1 sprig parsley, chopped
- 5 tablespoons butter
- 1/4 teaspoon salt
- 1/4 teaspoon pepper

Directions:

1. In a large skillet, cook bacon over medium heat until crisp, stirring occasionally. Remove with a slotted spoon; drain on paper towels. Discard drippings, reserving 1-1/2 teaspoons in the pan. Add onion to drippings; cook and stir over medium-high heat until tender.
2. Meanwhile, place all ingredients Bring to a boil over high heat. Reduce heat to medium; cook, uncovered, 10-15 minutes or until tender. Reserve 1 cup potato water.
3. Add milk, salt and pepper to the saucepan; heat through. Stir in bacon and onion.

Nutrition Info:

- Per Servings 5.4g Carbs, 10g Protein, 31.9g Fat, 322 Calories

Quail Eggs And Winter Melon Soup

Servings: 6 | Cooking Time: 40 Minutes

Ingredients:

- 1-pound pork bones
- 4 cloves of garlic, minced
- 1 onion, chopped
- 1 winter melon, peeled and sliced
- 10 quail eggs, pre-boiled and peeled
- Pepper and salt to taste
- 6 cups water, divided
- Chopped cilantro for garnish (optional)

Directions:

1. Place a heavy-bottomed pot on medium-high fire.
2. Add 5 cups water and pork bones. Season generously with pepper.
3. Bring to a boil, lower fire to a simmer, cover and cook for 30 minutes. Discard bones.
4. Add remaining ingredients except for the cilantro. Cover and simmer for another 10 minutes.
5. Adjust seasoning to taste.
6. Serve and enjoy with cilantro for garnish.

Nutrition Info:

- Per Servings 5.6g Carbs, 4.0g Protein, 3.0g Fat, 65 Calories

Grilled Steak Salad With Pickled Peppers

Servings: 4 | Cooking Time: 15 Minutes

Ingredients:

- 1 lb skirt steak, sliced
- Salt and black pepper to season
- 1 tsp olive oil
- 1 ½ cups mixed salad greens
- 3 chopped pickled peppers
- 2 tbsp red wine vinaigrette
- ½ cup crumbled queso fresco

Directions:

1. Brush the steak slices with olive oil and season with salt and pepper on both sides.
2. Heat frying pan over high heat and cook the steaks on each side to the desired doneness, for about 5-6 minutes. Remove to a bowl, cover and leave to rest while you make the salad.
3. Mix the salad greens, pickled peppers, and vinaigrette in a salad bowl. Add the beef and sprinkle with cheese. Serve the salad with roasted parsnips.

Nutrition Info:

- Per Servings 2g Carbs, 18g Protein, 26g Fat, 315 Calories

Spicy Chicken Bean Soup

Servings: 8 | Cooking Time:1h 20 Mins

Ingredients:

- 8 skinless, boneless chicken breast halves
- 5 cubes chicken bouillon
- 2 cans peeled and diced tomatoes
- 1 container sour cream
- 1 cups frozen cut green beans
- 3 tablespoons. olive oil
- Salt and black pepper to taste
- 1 onion, chopped
- 3 cloves garlic, chopped
- 1 cups frozen cut green beans

Directions:

1. Heat olive oil in a large pot over medium heat, add onion, garlic and cook until tender. Stir in water, chicken, salt, pepper, bouillon cubes and bring to boil, simmer for 1 hour on Low. Remove chicken from the pot, reserve 5 cups broth and slice.
2. Stir in the remaining ingredients in the pot and simmer 30 minutes. Serve and enjoy.

Nutrition Info:

- Per Servings 7.6g Carbs, 26.5g Protein, 15.3g Fat, 275.1 Calories

Green Minestrone Soup

Servings: 4 | Cooking Time: 25 Minutes

Ingredients:

- 2 tbsp ghee
- 2 tbsp onion garlic puree
- 2 heads broccoli, cut in florets
- 2 stalks celery, chopped
- 5 cups vegetable broth
- 1 cup baby spinach
- Salt and black pepper to taste

Directions:

1. Melt the ghee in a saucepan over medium heat and sauté the garlic for 3 minutes until softened. Mix in the broccoli and celery, and cook for 4 minutes until slightly tender. Pour in the broth, bring to a boil, then reduce the heat to medium-low and simmer covered for about 5 minutes.
2. Drop in the spinach to wilt, adjust the seasonings, and cook for 4 minutes. Ladle soup into serving bowls. Serve with a sprinkle of grated Gruyere cheese and freshly baked low carb carrot bread.

Nutrition Info:

- Per Servings 2g Carbs, 8g Protein, 20.3g Fat, 227 Calories

Chicken Stock And Green Bean Soup

Servings: 6 | Cooking Time:1h 30 Mins

Ingredients:

- 2 tablespoons butter
- 1/2 onion, diced
- 2 ribs celery, diced
- 1 cup green beans
- 6 bacon slices
- What you'll need from the store cupboard:
- 3 cloves garlic, sliced
- 1 quart chicken stock
- 2 1/2 cups water
- 1 bay leaf
- Salt and ground black pepper to taste

Directions:

1. In a large pot over medium-low heat, melt the butter. Add the onions, celery, and sliced garlic, cook for 5-8 minutes, or until onions are soft.
2. Stir in in bacon slices, bay leaf, and green beans. Add chicken stock and water, stirring until well combined, and simmer for 1 hour and 15 minutes, or green beans are soft. Sprinkle with salt and black pepper before serving.

Nutrition Info:

- Per Servings 7g Carbs, 15.1g Protein, 11.3g Fat, 208.6 Calories

Tomato Hamburger Soup

Servings: 8 | Cooking Time: 25 Minutes

Ingredients:

- 1-pound ground beef
- 1 can V-8 juice
- 2 packages frozen vegetable mix
- 1 can condensed mushroom soup
- 2 teaspoon dried onion powder
- 5 tablespoons olive oil
- Salt and pepper to taste
- 1 cup water

Directions:

1. Place a pot over medium flame and heat for 2 minutes. Add oil and heat for a minute.
2. Sauté the beef until lightly browned, around 7 minutes. Season with salt, pepper, and onion powder.
3. Add the mushroom soup and water.
4. Give a good stir to combine everything.
5. Cover and bring to a boil, lower fire to a simmer and cook for 10 minutes.
6. Stir in vegetables. Cook until heated through around 5 minutes. Adjust seasoning if needed.
7. Serve and enjoy.

Nutrition Info:

- Per Servings 10g Carbs, 18.1g Protein, 14.8g Fat, 227 Calories

Citrusy Brussels Sprouts Salad

Servings: 6 | Cooking Time: 3 Minutes

Ingredients:

- 2 tablespoons olive oil
- ¾ pound Brussels sprouts
- 1 cup walnuts
- Juice from 1 lemon
- ½ cup grated parmesan cheese
- Salt and pepper to taste

Directions:

1. Heat oil in a skillet over medium flame and sauté the Brussels sprouts for 3 minutes until slightly wilted. Removed from heat and allow to cool.
2. In a bowl, toss together the cooled Brussels sprouts and the rest of the ingredients.
3. Toss to coat.

Nutrition Info:

- Per Servings 8g Carbs, 6g Protein, 23g Fat, 259 Calories

Balsamic Cucumber Salad

Servings: 6 | Cooking Time: 0 Minutes

Ingredients:

- 1 large English cucumber, halved and sliced
- 1 cup grape tomatoes, halved
- 1 medium red onion, sliced thinly
- ¼ cup balsamic vinaigrette
- ¾ cup feta cheese
- Salt and pepper to taste
- ¼ cup olive oil

Directions:

1. Place all ingredients in a bowl.
2. Toss to coat everything with the dressing.
3. Allow chilling before serving.

Nutrition Info:

- Per Servings 9g Carbs, 4.8g Protein, 16.7g Fat, 253 Calories

Spinach Fruit Salad With Seeds

Servings: 4 | Cooking Time: 1 Hour 10 Minutes

Ingredients:

- 2 tablespoons sesame seeds
- 1 tablespoon poppy seeds
- 1 tablespoon minced onion
- 10 ounces fresh spinach - rinsed, dried and torn into bite-size pieces
- 1 quart strawberries - cleaned, hulled and sliced
- 1/2 cup stevia
- 1/2 cup olive oil
- 1/4 cup distilled white vinegar
- 1/4 teaspoon Worcestershire sauce
- 1/4 teaspoon paprika

Directions:

1. Mix together the spinach and strawberry in a large bowl, stir in the sesame seeds, poppy seeds, stevia, olive oil, vinegar, paprika, Worcestershire sauce and onion in a medium bowl. Cover and cool for 1 hour.
2. Pour dressing over salad to combine well. Serve immediately or refrigerate for 15 minutes.

Nutrition Info:

- Per Servings 8.6g Carbs, 6g Protein, 18g Fat, 220 Calories

Corn And Bacon Chowder

Servings: 8 | Cooking Time: 23 Minutes

Ingredients:

- ½ cup bacon, fried and crumbled
- 1 package celery, onion, and bell pepper mix
- 2 cups full-fat milk
- ½ cup sharp cheddar cheese, grated
- 5 tablespoons butter
- Pepper and salt to taste
- 1 cup water

Directions:

1. In a heavy-bottomed pot, melt butter.
2. Saute the bacon and celery for 3 minutes.
3. Turn fire on to medium. Add remaining ingredients and cook for 20 minutes until thick.
4. Serve and enjoy with a sprinkle of crumbled bacon.

Nutrition Info:

- Per Servings 4.4g Carbs, 16.6g Protein, 13.6g Fat, 210.5 Calories

Cobb Egg Salad In Lettuce Cups

Servings: 4 | Cooking Time: 20 Minutes

Ingredients:

- 2 chicken breasts, cut into pieces
- 1 tbsp olive oil
- Salt and black pepper to season
- 6 large eggs
- 1 ½ cups water
- 2 tomatoes, seeded, chopped
- 6 tbsp Greek yogurt
- 1 head green lettuce, firm leaves removed for cups

Directions:

1. Preheat oven to 400ºF. Put the chicken pieces in a bowl, drizzle with olive oil, and sprinkle with salt and black pepper. Mix the ingredients until the chicken is well coated with the seasoning.
2. Put the chicken on a prepared baking sheet and spread out evenly. Slide the baking sheet in the oven and bake the chicken until cooked through and golden brown for 8 minutes, turning once.
3. Bring the eggs to boil in salted water in a pot over medium heat for 6 minutes. Run the eggs in cold water, peel, and chop into small pieces. Transfer to a salad bowl.
4. Remove the chicken from the oven when ready and add to the salad bowl. Include the tomatoes and Greek yogurt; mix evenly with a spoon. Layer two lettuce leaves each as cups and fill with two tablespoons of egg salad each. Serve with chilled blueberry juice.

Nutrition Info:

- Per Servings 4g Carbs, 21g Protein, 24.5g Fat, 325 Calories

Bacon Tomato Salad

Servings: 6 | Cooking Time: 0 Minutes

Ingredients:

- 6 ounces iceberg lettuce blend
- 2 cups grape tomatoes, halved
- ¾ cup coleslaw salad dressing
- ¾ cup cheddar cheese, shredded
- 12 bacon strips, cooked and crumbled
- Salt and pepper to taste

Directions:

1. Put the lettuce and tomatoes in a salad bowl.
2. Drizzle with the dressing and sprinkle with cheese. Season with salt and pepper to taste then mix.
3. Garnish with bacon bits on top.

Nutrition Info:

- Per Servings 8g Carbs, 10g Protein, 20g Fat, 268 Calories

Fruit Salad With Poppy Seeds

Servings: 5 | Cooking Time: 25 Mins

Ingredients:

- 1 tablespoon poppy seeds
- 1 head romaine lettuce, torn into bite-size pieces
- 4 ounces shredded Swiss cheese
- 1 avocado- peeled, cored and diced
- 2 teaspoons diced onion
- 1/2 cup lemon juice
- 1/2 cup stevia
- 1/2 teaspoon salt
- 2/3 cup olive oil
- 1 teaspoon Dijon style prepared mustard

Directions:

1. Combine stevia, lemon juice, onion, mustard, and salt in a blender. Process until well blended.
2. Add oil until mixture is thick and smooth. Add poppy seeds, stir just a few seconds or more to mix.
3. In a large serving bowl, toss together the remaining ingredients.
4. Pour dressing over salad just before serving, and toss to coat.

Nutrition Info:

- Per Servings 6g Carbs, 4.9g Protein, 20.6g Fat, 277 Calories

Beef Reuben Soup

Servings: 6 | Cooking Time: 20 Minutes

Ingredients:

- 1 onion, diced
- 6 cups beef stock
- 1 tsp caraway seeds
- 2 celery stalks, diced
- 2 garlic cloves, minced
- 2 cups heavy cream
- 1 cup sauerkraut
- 1 pound corned beef, chopped
- 3 tbsp butter
- 1 ½ cup swiss cheese
- Salt and black pepper, to taste

Directions:

1. Melt the butter in a large pot. Add onion and celery, and fry for 3 minutes until tender. Add garlic and cook for another minute.
2. Pour the beef stock over and stir in sauerkraut, salt, caraway seeds, and add a pinch of pepper. Bring to a boil. Reduce the heat to low, and add the corned beef. Cook for about 15 minutes, adjust the seasoning. Stir in heavy cream and cheese and cook for 1 minute.

Nutrition Info:

- Per Servings 8g Carbs, 23g Protein, 37g Fat, 450 Calories

Pesto Tomato Cucumber Salad

Servings: 8 | Cooking Time: 0 Minutes

Ingredients:

- ½ cup Italian salad dressing
- ¼ cup prepared pesto
- 3 large tomatoes, sliced
- 2 medium cucumbers, halved and sliced
- 1 small red onion, sliced
- Salt and pepper to taste
- 3 tablespoons olive oil

Directions:

1. In a bowl, whisk the salad dressing and pesto. Season with salt and pepper to taste.
2. Toss gently to incorporate everything.
3. Refrigerate before serving.

Nutrition Info:

- Per Servings 3.7g Carbs, 1.8g Protein, 12g Fat, 128 Calories

Pesto Arugula Salad

Servings: 4 | Cooking Time: 10 Minutes

Ingredients:

- ¾ cup red peppers, seeded and chopped
- ¾ cup commercial basil pesto
- 1 small mozzarella cheese ball, diced
- 3 handfuls of arugulas, washed
- Salt and pepper to taste
- 5 tablespoons olive oil

Directions:

1. Mix all ingredients in a salad bowl and toss to coat.
2. Season with salt and pepper to taste.

Nutrition Info:

- Per Servings 2.8g Carbs, 6.7g Protein, 20g Fat, 214 Calories

Bacon And Spinach Salad

Servings: 4 | Cooking Time: 20 Minutes

Ingredients:

- 2 large avocados, 1 chopped and 1 sliced
- 1 spring onion, sliced
- 4 cooked bacon slices, crumbled
- 2 cups spinach
- 2 small lettuce heads, chopped
- 2 hard-boiled eggs, chopped
- Vinaigrette:
- 3 tbsp olive oil
- 1 tsp Dijon mustard
- 1 tbsp apple cider vinegar

Directions:

1. Combine the spinach, lettuce, eggs, chopped avocado, and spring onion, in a large bowl. Whisk together the vinaigrette ingredients in another bowl.
2. Pour the dressing over, toss to combine and top with the sliced avocado and bacon.

Nutrition Info:

- Per Servings 3.4g Carbs, 7g Protein, 33g Fat, 350 Calories

Creamy Squash Bisque

Servings: 8 | Cooking Time: 25 Minutes

Ingredients:

- ½ tablespoon turmeric powder
- ½ teaspoon cumin
- ½ cup onion, chopped
- 2 medium-sized kabocha squash, seeded and chopped
- 1 cup coconut milk
- 3 tablespoons oil
- 1 cup water
- Pepper and salt to taste

Directions:

1. Place a heavy-bottomed pot on medium-high fire and heat for 3 minutes.
2. Add oil to the pot and swirl to coat sides and bottom of the pot. Heat for 2 minutes.
3. Place squash in a single layer and season generously with pepper and salt.
4. Sprinkle turmeric, cumin, and onion. Add water.
5. Cover and bring to a boil. Once boiling, lower fire to a simmer and let it cook for 10 minutes.
6. With a handheld blender, puree squash. Stir in coconut milk and mix well. Cook until heated through, around 5 minutes.
7. Serve and enjoy.

Nutrition Info:

- Per Servings 10.9g Carbs, 3.1g Protein, 18.1g Fat, 218 Calories

Crunchy And Salty Cucumber

Servings: 4 | Cooking Time: 0 Minutes

Ingredients:

- 2 Persian cucumbers, sliced thinly
- 1 medium radish, trimmed and sliced thinly
- Juice from 1 lemon
- ½ cup parmesan cheese, shredded
- A dash of flaky sea salt
- A dash of ground black pepper
- 5 tablespoons olive oil

Directions:

1. Place all vegetables in a bowl.
2. Stir in the lemon juice and parmesan cheese.
3. Season with salt and pepper to taste
4. Add olive oil or salad oil.
5. Toss to mix everything.

Nutrition Info:

- Per Servings 4g Carbs, 3.7g Protein, 20g Fat, 209 Calories

Salmon Salad With Walnuts

Servings: 2 | Cooking Time: 10 Minutes

Ingredients:

- 2 salmon fillets
- 2 tablespoons balsamic vinaigrette, divided
- 1/8 teaspoon pepper
- 2 cups mixed salad greens
- 1/4 cup walnuts
- 2 tablespoons crumbled cheese
- Salt and pepper to taste
- 3 tablespoons olive oil

Directions:

1. Brush the salmon with half of the balsamic vinaigrette and sprinkle with pepper.
2. Grill the salmon over medium heat for 5 minutes on each side.
3. Crumble the salmon and place in a mixing bowl. Add the rest of the ingredients and season with salt and pepper to taste.

Nutrition Info:

- Per Servings 8g Carbs, 5g Protein, 30g Fat, 313 Calories

Mexican Soup

Servings: 4 | Cooking Time: 25 Minutes

Ingredients:

- 1-pound boneless skinless chicken thighs, cut into 3/4-inch pieces
- 1 tablespoon reduced-sodium taco seasoning
- 1 cup salsa
- 1 carton reduced-sodium chicken broth
- 4 tablespoons olive oil

Directions:

1. In a large saucepan, heat oil over medium-high heat. Add chicken; cook and stir 6-8 minutes or until no longer pink. Stir in taco seasoning.
2. Add remaining ingredients; bring to a boil. Reduce heat; simmer, uncovered, 5 minutes to allow flavors to blend. Skim fat before serving.

Nutrition Info:

- Per Servings 5.6g Carbs, 25g Protein, 16.5g Fat, 281 Calories

Chapter 8 Desserts And Drinks Recipes

Chapter 8 Desserts And Drinks Recipes

Coffee Fat Bombs

Servings: 6 | Cooking Time: 3 Minutes + Cooling Time

Ingredients:

- 1 ½ cups mascarpone cheese
- ½ cup melted butter
- 3 tbsp unsweetened cocoa powder
- ¼ cup erythritol
- 6 tbsp brewed coffee, room temperature

Directions:

1. Whisk the mascarpone cheese, butter, cocoa powder, erythritol, and coffee with a hand mixer until creamy and fluffy, for 1 minute. Fill into muffin tins and freeze for 3 hours until firm.

Nutrition Info:

- Per Servings 2g Carbs, 4g Protein, 14g Fat, 145 Calories

No Nuts Fudge

Servings: 15 | Cooking Time: 4 Hours

Ingredients:

- ¼ cup cocoa powder
- ½ teaspoon baking powder
- 1 stick of butter, melted
- 4 tablespoons erythritol
- 6 eggs, beaten
- Salt to taste.

Directions:

1. Mix all ingredients in a slow cooker.
2. Add a pinch of salt.
3. Mix until well combined.
4. Cover pot.
5. Press the low settings and adjust the time to 4 hours.

Nutrition Info:

- Per Servings 1.3g Carbs, 4.3g Protein, 12.2g Fat, 132 Calories

Cinnamon Cookies

Servings: 4 | Cooking Time: 25 Minutes

Ingredients:

- 2 cups almond flour
- ½ tsp baking soda
- ¾ cup sweetener
- ½ cup butter, softened
- A pinch of salt
- Coating:
- 2 tbsp erythritol sweetener
- 1 tsp cinnamon

Directions:

1. Preheat your oven to 350ºF. Combine all cookie ingredients in a bowl. Make 16 balls out of the mixture and flatten them with hands. Combine the cinnamon and erythritol. Dip the cookies in the cinnamon mixture and arrange them on a lined cookie sheet. Cook for 15 minutes, until crispy.

Nutrition Info:

- Per Servings 1.5g Carbs, 3g Protein, 13g Fat, 131 Calories

Nutritiously Green Milk Shake

Servings: 1 | Cooking Time: 5 Minutes

Ingredients:

- 1 cup coconut cream
- 1 packet Stevia, or more to taste
- 1 tbsp coconut flakes, unsweetened
- 2 cups spring mix salad
- 3 tbsps coconut oil
- 1 cup water

Directions:

1. Add all ingredients in a blender.
2. Blend until smooth and creamy.
3. Serve and enjoy.

Nutrition Info:

- Per Servings 10g Carbs, 10.5g Protein, 95.3g Fat, 887 Calories

Almond Choco Shake

Servings: 1 | Cooking Time: 0 Minutes

Ingredients:

- ½ cup heavy cream, liquid
- 1 tbsp cocoa powder
- 1 packet Stevia, or more to taste
- 5 almonds, chopped
- 1 ½ cups water
- 3 tbsp coconut oil

Directions:

1. Add all ingredients in a blender.
2. Blend until smooth and creamy.
3. Serve and enjoy.

Nutrition Info:

- Per Servings 9.7g Carbs, 11.9g Protein, 45.9g Fat, 485 Calories

Lemon Gummies

Servings: 4 | Cooking Time: 15 Minutes

Ingredients:

- 1/4 cup fresh lemon juice
- 2 Tablespoons gelatin powder
- 2 Tablespoons stevia, to taste
- ½ cup half and half
- 1 Tablespoon water

Directions:

1. In a small saucepan, heat up water and lemon juice.
2. Slowly stir in the gelatin powder and the rest of the ingredients. Heating and mixing well until dissolved.
3. Pour into silicone molds.
4. Freeze or refrigerate for 2+ hours until firm.

Nutrition Info:

- Per Servings 1.0g Carbs, 3.0g Protein, 7g Fat, 88 Calories

Coconut Macadamia Nut Bombs

Servings: 4 | Cooking Time: 0 Mins

Ingredients:

- 2 packets stevia
- 5 tbsps unsweetened coconut powder
- 10 tbsps coconut oil
- 3 tbsps chopped macadamia nuts
- Salt to taste

Directions:

1. Heat the coconut oil in a pan over medium heat. Add coconut powder, stevia and salt, stirring to combined well; then remove from heat.
2. Spoon mixture into a lined mini muffin pan. Place in the freezer for a few hours.
3. Sprinkle nuts over the mixture before serving.

Nutrition Info:

- Per Servings 0.2g Carbs, 1.1g Protein, 15.2g Fat, 143 Calories

Minty-coco And Greens Shake

Servings: 1 | Cooking Time: 0 Minutes

Ingredients:

- ½ cup coconut milk
- 2 peppermint leaves
- 2 packets Stevia, or as needed
- 1 cup 50/50 salad mix
- 1 tbsp coconut oil
- 1 ½ cups water

Directions:

1. Add all ingredients in a blender.
2. Blend until smooth and creamy.
3. Serve and enjoy.

Nutrition Info:

- Per Servings 5.8g Carbs, 2.7g Protein, 37.8g Fat, 344 Calories

Granny Smith Apple Tart

Servings: 8 | Cooking Time: 65 Minutes

Ingredients:

- 6 tbsp butter
- 2 cups almond flour
- 1 tsp cinnamon
- ⅓ cup sweetener
- Filling:
- 2 cups sliced Granny Smith
- ¼ cup butter
- ¼ cup sweetener
- ½ tsp cinnamon
- ½ tsp lemon juice
- Topping:
- ¼ tsp cinnamon
- 2 tbsp sweetener

Directions:

1. Preheat your oven to 370°F and combine all crust ingredients in a bowl. Press this mixture into the bottom of a greased pan. Bake for 5 minutes.
2. Meanwhile, combine the apples and lemon juice in a bowl and let them sit until the crust is ready. Arrange them on top of the crust. Combine the rest of the filling ingredients, and brush this mixture over the apples. Bake for about 30 minutes.
3. Press the apples down with a spatula, return to oven, and bake for 20 more minutes. Combine the cinnamon and sweetener, in a bowl, and sprinkle over the tart.
4. Note: Granny Smith apples have just 9.5g of net carbs per 100g. Still high for you? Substitute with Chayote squash, which has the same texture and rich nutrients, and just around 4g of net carbs .

Nutrition Info:

- Per Servings 6.7g Carbs, 7g Protein, 26g Fat, 302 Calories

Coco-loco Creamy Shake

Servings: 1 | Cooking Time: 0 Minutes

Ingredients:

- ½ cup coconut milk
- 2 tbsp Dutch-processed cocoa powder, unsweetened
- 1 cup brewed coffee, chilled
- 1 tbsp hemp seeds
- 1-2 packets Stevia
- 3 tbsps MCT oil or coconut oil

Directions:

1. Add all ingredients in a blender.
2. Blend until smooth and creamy.
3. Serve and enjoy.

Nutrition Info:

- Per Servings 10.2g Carbs, 5.4g Protein, 61.1g Fat, 567 Calories

Strawberry-coconut Shake

Servings: 1 | Cooking Time: 0 Minutes

Ingredients:

- ½ cup whole milk yogurt
- 3 tbsp MCT oil
- ¼ cup strawberries, chopped
- 1 tbsp coconut flakes, unsweetened
- 1 tbsp hemp seeds
- 1 ½ cups water
- 1 packet Stevia, or more to taste

Directions:

1. Add all ingredients in a blender.
2. Blend until smooth and creamy.
3. Serve and enjoy.

Nutrition Info:

- Per Servings 10.2g Carbs, 6.4g Protein, 50.9g Fat, 511 Calories

Strawberry And Yogurt Smoothie

Servings: 3 | Cooking Time: 5 Minutes

Ingredients:

- 1/2 cup yogurt
- 1 cup strawberries
- 1 teaspoon almond milk
- 1 teaspoon lime juice
- 1 1/2 teaspoons stevia

Directions:

1. Place all ingredients in a blender, blender until finely smooth. Serve and enjoy.

Nutrition Info:

- Per Servings 6.3g Carbs, 4.6g Protein, 12.4g Fat, 155.2 Calories

Creamy Choco Shake

Servings: 1 | Cooking Time: 0 Minutes

Ingredients:

- ½ cup heavy cream
- 2 tbsp cocoa powder
- 1 packet Stevia, or more to taste
- 1 cup water
- 3 tbsps coconut oil

Directions:

1. Add all ingredients in a blender.
2. Blend until smooth and creamy.
3. Serve and enjoy.

Nutrition Info:

- Per Servings 7.9g Carbs, 3.2g Protein, 64.6g Fat, 582 Calories

Smarties Cookies

Servings: 8 | Cooking Time: 10 Mins

Ingredients:

- 1/4 cup. butter
- 1/2 cup. almond flour
- 1 tsp. vanilla essence
- 12 oz. bag of smarties
- 1 cup. stevia
- 1/4 tsp. baking powder

Directions:

1. Sift in flour and baking powder in a bowl, then stir through butter and mix until well combined.
2. Whisk in stevia and vanilla essence , stir until thick.
3. Then add the smarties and use your hand to mix and divide into small balls.
4. Bake until completely cooked, about 10 minutes. Let it cool and serve.

Nutrition Info:

- Per Servings 20.77g Carbs, 3.7g Protein, 11.89g Fat, 239 Calories

Dark Chocolate Mochaccino Ice Bombs

Servings: 4 | Cooking Time: 2 Hours And 10 Minutes

Ingredients:

- ½ pound cream cheese
- 4 tbsp powdered sweetener
- 2 ounces strong coffee
- 2 tbsp cocoa powder, unsweetened
- 1 ounce cocoa butter, melted
- 2 ½ ounces dark chocolate, melted

Directions:

1. Combine cream cheese, sweetener, coffee, and cocoa powder, in a food processor. Roll 2 tbsp. of the mixture and place on a lined tray.
2. Mix the melted cocoa butter and chocolate, and coat the bombs with it. Freeze for 2 hours.

Nutrition Info:

- Per Servings 1.4g Carbs, 1.9g Protein, 13g Fat, 127 Calories

Strawberry And Basil Lemonade

Servings: 4 | Cooking Time: 3 Minutes

Ingredients:

- 4 cups water
- 12 strawberries, leaves removed
- 1 cup fresh lemon juice
- ⅓ cup fresh basil
- ¾ cup swerve
- Crushed Ice
- Halved strawberries to garnish
- Basil leaves to garnish

Directions:

1. Spoon some ice into 4 serving glasses and set aside. In a pitcher, add the water, strawberries, lemon juice, basil, and swerve. Insert the blender and process the ingredients for 30 seconds.
2. The mixture should be pink and the basil finely chopped. Adjust the taste and add the ice in the glasses. Drop 2 strawberry halves and some basil in each glass and serve immediately.

Nutrition Info:

- Per Servings 5.8g Carbs, 0.7g Protein, 0.1g Fat, 66 Calories

Strawberry Vanilla Extract Smoothie

Servings: 3 | Cooking Time: 5 Mins

Ingredients:

- 1 cup almond milk
- 14 frozen strawberries
- 1 1/2 teaspoons stevia
- What you'll need from the store cupboard:
- 1/2 teaspoon vanilla extract

Directions:

1. Place almond milk and strawberries in a blender, blend until creamy. Add vanilla and stevia if desired, blend again and serve.

Nutrition Info:

- Per Servings 5g Carbs, 12.8g Protein, 18.8g Fat, 240.4 Calories

Hazelnut-lettuce Yogurt Shake

Servings: 1 | Cooking Time: 0 Minutes

Ingredients:

- 1 cup whole milk yogurt
- 1 cup lettuce chopped
- 1 tbsp Hazelnut chopped
- 1 packet Stevia, or more to taste
- 1 tbsp olive oil
- 1 cup water

Directions:

1. Add all ingredients in a blender.
2. Blend until smooth and creamy.
3. Serve and enjoy.

Nutrition Info:

- Per Servings 8.8g Carbs, 9.4g Protein, 22.2g Fat, 282 Calories

Sea Salt 'n Macadamia Choco Barks

Servings: 10 | Cooking Time: 5 Minutes

Ingredients:

- 1 teaspoon sea salt flakes
- 1/4 cup macadamia nuts, crushed
- 2 Tablespoons erythritol or stevia, to taste
- 3.5 oz 100% dark chocolate, broken into pieces
- 2 Tablespoons coconut oil, melted

Directions:

1. Melt the chocolate and coconut oil over a very low heat.
2. Remove from heat. Stir in sweetener.
3. Pour the mixture into a loaf pan and place in the fridge for 15 minutes.
4. Scatter the crushed macadamia nuts on top along with the sea salt. Lightly press into the chocolate.
5. Place back into the fridge or freezer for 2 hours.

Nutrition Info:

- Per Servings 1.0g Carbs, 2.0g Protein, 8.0g Fat, 84 Calories

Strawberry-choco Shake

Servings: 1 | Cooking Time: 0 Minutes

Ingredients:

- ½ cup heavy cream, liquid
- 1 tbsp cocoa powder
- 1 packet Stevia, or more to taste
- 4 strawberries, sliced
- 1 tbsp coconut flakes, unsweetened
- 1 ½ cups water
- 3 tbsps coconut oil

Directions:

1. Add all ingredients in a blender.
2. Blend until smooth and creamy.
3. Serve and enjoy.

Nutrition Info:

- Per Servings 10.1g Carbs, 2.6g Protein, 65.3g Fat, 610 Calories

Raspberry And Greens Shake

Servings: 1 | Cooking Time: 0 Minutes

Ingredients:

- ½ cup half and half
- 1 packet Stevia, or more to taste
- 4 raspberries, fresh
- 1 tbsp macadamia oil
- 1 cup Spinach
- 1 cup water

Directions:

1. Add all ingredients in a blender.
2. Blend until smooth and creamy.
3. Serve and enjoy.

Nutrition Info:

- Per Servings 2.7g Carbs, 1.4g Protein, 15.5g Fat, 151 Calories

Chia And Blackberry Pudding

Servings: 2 | Cooking Time: 10 Minutes

Ingredients:

- 1 cup full-fat natural yogurt
- 2 tsp swerve
- 2 tbsp chia seeds
- 1 cup fresh blackberries
- 1 tbsp lemon zest
- Mint leaves, to serve

Directions:

1. Mix together the yogurt and the swerve. Stir in the chia seeds. Reserve 4 blackberries for garnish and mash the remaining ones with a fork until pureed. Stir in the yogurt mixture
2. Chill in the fridge for 30 minutes. When cooled, divide the mixture between 2 glasses. Top each with a couple of raspberries, mint leaves, lemon zest and serve.

Nutrition Info:

- Per Servings 4.7g Carbs, 7.5g Protein, 10g Fat, 169 Calories

Lime Strawberry Smoothie

Servings: 3 | Cooking Time: 3 Mins

Ingredients:

- 4 ice cubes
- 1/4 fresh strawberry
- 1 large avocado, diced
- 1 cup lime juice

Directions:

1. In a food processor, combine all ingredients and puree on High until a smooth smoothie is formed. Serve and enjoy.

Nutrition Info:

- Per Servings 4g Carbs, 3g Protein, 11g Fat, 127 Calories

Blueberry And Greens Smoothie

Servings: 1 | Cooking Time: 0 Minutes

Ingredients:

- ¼ cup coconut milk
- 2 tbsps blueberries
- ½ cup arugula
- 1 tbsp hemp seeds
- 2 packets Stevia, or as needed
- 1 ½ cups water
- 3 tbsps coconut oil

Directions:

1. Add all ingredients in a blender.
2. Blend until smooth and creamy.
3. Serve and enjoy.

Nutrition Info:

- Per Servings 10.4g Carbs, 3.6g Protein, 59.8g Fat, 572 Calories

Cranberry White Chocolate Barks

Servings: 6 | Cooking Time: 5 Minutes

Ingredients:

- 10 oz unsweetened white chocolate, chopped
- ½ cup erythritol
- ⅓ cup dried cranberries, chopped
- ⅓ cup toasted walnuts, chopped
- ¼ tsp pink salt

Directions:

1. Line a baking sheet with parchment paper. Pour chocolate and erythritol in a bowl, and melt in the microwave for 25 seconds, stirring three times until fully melted. Stir in the cranberries, walnuts, and salt, reserving a few cranberries and walnuts for garnishing.
2. Pour the mixture on the baking sheet and spread out. Sprinkle with remaining cranberries and walnuts. Refrigerate for 2 hours to set. Break into bite-size pieces to serve.

Nutrition Info:

- Per Servings 3g Carbs, 6g Protein, 21g Fat, 225 Calories

21 Day Meal Plan

	Breakfast	Lunch	Dinner
Day 1	Parmesan Crackers With Guacamole	Creamy Vegetable Stew	Tofu Sesame Skewers With Warm Kale Salad
Day 2	Herb Cheese Sticks	Butternut Squash And Cauliflower Stew	Creamy Cucumber Avocado Soup
Day 3	Coconut And Chocolate Bars	Wild Mushroom And Asparagus Stew	Zesty Frittata With Roasted Chilies
Day 4	Italian-style Chicken Wraps	Brussels Sprouts With Tofu	Sriracha Tofu With Yogurt Sauce
Day 5	Keto "cornbread"	Stir Fried Broccoli 'n Chicken	Creamy Artichoke And Spinach
Day 6	Curry ' N Poppy Devilled Eggs	Chili Lime Chicken	Fall Roasted Vegetables
Day 7	Chocolate Mousse	Chicken Wings With Thyme Chutney	Coconut Chicken Soup
Day 8	Mascarpone Snapped Amaretti Biscuits	Spicy Chicken Kabobs	Chicken Breasts With Cheddar & Pepperoni
Day 9	Keto Enchilada Bake	Chicken In Creamy Mushroom Sauce	Slow-cooked Mexican Turkey Soup
Day 10	Vegan Mushroom Pizza	Turkey, Coconut And Kale Chili	Yummy Chicken Nuggets
Day 11	Kale Cheese Waffles	Almond-crusted Chicken Breasts	Bacon And Spinach Salad

	Breakfast	Lunch	Dinner
Day 12	Onion & Nuts Stuffed Mushrooms	Baked Chicken Pesto	Turkey & Leek Soup
Day 13	Portobello Mushroom Burgers	Garlic Pork Chops	Easy Tomato Salad
Day 14	Yummy Chicken Queso	Avocado Cheese Pepper Chicken	Butternut And Kale Soup
Day 15	Creamy Squash Bisque	Easy Thai 5-spice Pork Stew	Watermelon And Cucumber Salad
Day 16	Salmon Salad With Walnuts	Greek Chicken With Capers	Bacon Chowder
Day 17	Cinnamon Cookies	New York Strip Steak With Mushroom Sauce	Quail Eggs And Winter Melon Soup
Day 18	Nutritiously Green Milk Shake	Hot Pork With Dill Pickles	Grilled Steak Salad With Pickled Peppers
Day 19	Almond Choco Shake	Beef Meatballs	Spicy Chicken Bean Soup
Day 20	Granny Smith Apple Tart	Slow Cooker Pork	Green Minestrone Soup
Day 21	Coco-loco Creamy Shake	Italian Sausage Stew	Chicken Stock And Green Bean Soup

Appendix : Recipes Index

C

D

E

F

G

H

I

Printed in Great Britain
by Amazon

19482837R00066